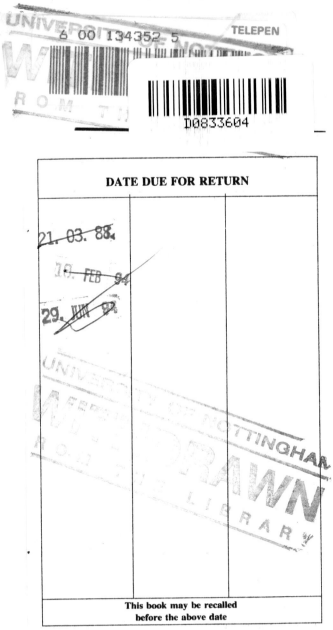

William of Glasshampton
FRIAR · MONK · SOLITARY

William of Glasshampton

FRIAR · MONK · SOLITARY

1862–1937

A record of his life
with selections from his letters
and from the
reminiscences of his friends

BY

Geoffrey Curtis, C.R.

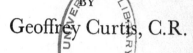

SECOND EDITION

with an Introduction by
the Guardian of Glasshampton

Brother Alban, S.S.F.

LONDON

SPCK

First published 1947
Second edition 1978
Reprinted 1978
SPCK
Holy Trinity Church
Marylebone Road
London NW1 4DU

Printed in Great Britain by
Biddles Ltd., Guildford, Surrey

ISBN 0 281 03570 9

CONTENTS

ACKNOWLEDGEMENTS vii

INTRODUCTION ix

PROLOGUE xiii

PART I. THE MAKING OF A PRIEST

I. BOYHOOD 1

II. LAY-APOSTOLATE AND PROFESSION 5

III. FIRST YEARS IN THE PRIESTHOOD . . . 13
Life in a Vauxhall " Model-dwelling "

PART II. FRIAR

IV. VOCATION TO THE RELIGIOUS LIFE 17
Society of the Divine Compassion

V. SUPERIOR OF THE SOCIETY 23
Work among the Unemployed

VI. CALL TO THE LIFE OF PRAYER 31
Homes of St. Giles for Lepers

VII. THE YEARS OF VIGIL 45

VIII. RETURN TO HANNINGFIELD 66
The Gate Opens

PART III. MONK

IX. GLASSHAMPTON: THE STABLE 75

X. THE MONASTERY OF ST. MARY AT THE CROSS, GLASS-
HAMPTON 95

XI. THE EPIPHANY OF GLASSHAMPTON . . . 113
Its Growing Influence and an Interruption

v

PART IV. SOLITARY

XII.	THE FRUITS OF SOLITUDE	131
XIII.	A SPIRITUAL GUIDE	141
XIV.	PERSONALITY AND CHARACTER	151
XV.	THE LAST YEARS	158
XVI.	THE RETURN HOME	165

APPENDICES

I.	A LETTER FROM GLASSHAMPTON, SPRING, 1933	166
II.	NOTE ON FATHER WILLIAM'S POSITION AS A RELIGIOUS	169
III.	THE FUTURE OF GLASSHAMPTON	172

EPILOGUE

BY THE REV. R. E. RAYNES, SUPERIOR OF THE
COMMUNITY OF THE RESURRECTION . . . 172

ACKNOWLEDGEMENTS

To this work, as to a village church of the Middle Ages, many craftsmen have contributed. This has necessarily entailed both enrichment and modification of the emphasis and perspective of the work as originally conceived. To two helpers it is specially indebted. The first (anonymous) is an old friend of Father William from London days, to whose able hands some of the later chapters owe almost everything. The second, Miss Lucy Menzies, to whose writings many readers are already indebted for increasing their knowledge of the great servants of God, did not know Father William in his lifetime, but has come to know and love him through assisting with this book. Her diligence greatly facilitated the task of selecting from the tremendous quantity of letters that have been sent us, and her advice on the form of the book and on the method of treatment the subject required has been invaluable. We have to thank many for sending their reminiscences of Father William: in particular Mr. Harry Sirr, Canon Herbert King, the Rev. Sidney King, the Rev. Gilbert Shaw, and Mother Clare. To the executors we owe permission to read and to quote from the Glasshampton papers, a collection of all the correspondence and memoranda bearing on the long and thorough probation of William's call to the contemplative life and on his liberation from the normal life of the Society of The Divine Compassion for this purpose. He preserved these papers carefully at Glasshampton with a view to further scrutiny of authority in the event of the growth of a community, and also for the benefit of that community itself.

We are grateful to all those who have lent us letters from Father William. But apart from the loan of letters, the kindness of every one of Father William's friends has been unforgettable. First of all we must thank his brethren of the Society of Divine Compassion. Their deep love and appreciation of Father William were at his passing given immediate expression in a memorable article by Father Andrew in the *Church Times*.

I have been conscious, in writing of Father William's relations with his community, that there are contexts of circumstances within the life of a community which no one from outside can fully understand. But we believe that they will welcome selections from letters touching upon that relationship. They form a spiritual journal of those difficult years during which they were faced with a problem of which their final solution, a decision of some importance for the future development of the religious life, was so generous and so wise. I thank the Superior of my own community for his epilogue which makes so clear the significance of Father William for the church of our time; the Society of St. John the Evangelist for permission to print a letter of Father Bull, their late Superior, and for other help; the Community of the Holy Name, the first and the last religious community to which he ministered, for help with regard to those early and latter days; the two sisterhoods in charge of the Homes of St. Giles at East Hanningfield; the monks and oblates of Nashdom Abbey, especially the late Dom Bernard Clements, O.S.B., and the Rev. Father Edward, O.S.B., Editor of *Laudate*; Miss Maisie Spens for her kindness in reading and correcting the proofs; the Community of the Servants of Christ for their interest and for their prayers.

There is much more to be said about Father William of Glasshampton. But this is not the place for it. And the time is not yet.

GEOFFREY CURTIS, C.R.

INTRODUCTION

THE village of Shrawley straggles along some two miles of a by-road between Holt Heath and Stourport in Worcestershire. The motorist passing in the direction of Stourport would scarcely glimpse a notice at the entrance to a rough drive, indicating that it leads to "Glasshampton Monastery". Were he to venture along the irregular surface of the drive he would pass between two cottages, perhaps wondering momentarily if he would be stopped and asked to show a pass, and would ascend a steep slope. Then a long redbrick building would be visible in the distance.

An eighteenth-century engraving of this same drive, by Thomas Nash, shows it leading straight between lines of thick trees to an elegant manor house. The trees have gone and the manor has vanished with scarcely any trace. But its stables remain, and it is this building which can now be seen there, turned by one man into a religious house for men, and still so used. In its garth, once the stable yard, repose the remains of its founder, William of Glasshampton.

In this fortieth year since his death the life which he led and wished to propagate may be better understood. An old lady who remembers the time of his arrival has written: "He was not very welcome when he first came . . . Rather queer! Funny kind of friends too!" But she can also say of a later encounter with him: "He was on his way to Kidderminster for his confession. He walked there and back, sixteen miles all told, and fasting too." What were hard-working country folk to make of a man who lived in a derelict stable in order to say his prayers? But they came to respect him and to love him.

In recent years we have seen those dissatisfied with the values and aspirations of Western society turn to mystics and holy men of the east. There has been an acute interest in the occult and the world of spirits and devils, in ancient wisdom and unwisdom, even in "gods" from outer space. Television has made the general public aware of the continued existence of monks, friars, and nuns, even if the impression is given that their numbers are dwindling, as in some cases they are, though in others they are increasing. But those who are engaged in the spiritual quest are less likely now to be met with blank incomprehension.

We all know the experience of acquiring things and finding that joy and satisfaction in them does not last, and of trying to gain more joy by looking for more and more. This does not only apply to material things. There are other riches to be sought for: honour, prestige, an important job, a good place to live in, exciting things to look forward to. These too become part of the scenery, satisfaction does not last, and there are awful moments when it seems that these things have not added a great deal to us as people, though it is difficult to admit this. Then, perhaps, unforeseen troubles and tragedies arise, and the things we have striven for do not seem to help us all that much. St. Paul "boasted" of his lineage, his up-bringing, his learning, his personal life, his distinction as a scholar, his virtue, only to say that he had learned to count these things as "garbage" (according to the NEB). He forsook them all, since he had come to know that all that was worth living for, and living by, was the knowledge of God's love and mercy.

If it is God we seek, God we desire, we can find the real value of everything. But we have to find our way through a great deal of illusion for the love of God to be a reality for us—not an ideal, not a wistful hope, but a reality we know, even if in our foolishness we lose it over and over again, and have to return to the point where the vision is clear, unclouded, and real. Then we see the value of God's gifts, the joy of being truly human, the splendour of the humanity which is ours. I do not think that any of us who have given ourselves to life in a religious community would have done so if we had not had some inkling of where true value lies, which puts everything else in its proper perspective. That is the poverty of spirit which is blessed. That was the significance of the life Father William lived at Glasshampton.

We who are his successors, the Society of Saint Francis, are pri-marily an active community, though our life is meant to be, in one aspect, a dedication to this vision of truth so that we are available to it. There are very different styles of life in our community; we do not all have the same particular concerns, but we have tried to put ourselves at God's disposal. Badly, it may be, inconsistently, unsteadily, but with some intention of living for God's sake. We are all damaged, we have our oddnesses and weaknesses as well as our particular strengths. We are fortunate if we know it, and take ourselves with our imperfections and angularities, as well as our strengths, to the God who accepts us and, because he does so, can help us to begin to accept ourselves. Not as we would like to be, but as we are, for it is from that point only that God can change us and make us grow. This we do not only for ourselves and for our own fulfilment, not only for each other, not only for those whom we seek to serve, but also as a witness that there is a God who calls us to his state of life. For ultimately we must say that while community life may be justified as useful for some, and that it does sometimes serve others, it would not have come into being without some sense that God does call us to it; that we do what we do in response to something that lies beyond us and which leads us on. This sense of being drawn by God may easily drop out of sight among the cares of caring, the agonies and depressions that overtake us all as we seek to bear those of others.

That is why Glasshampton, with its atmosphere of prayer and reflection, has an important place in our community life. Brethren spend some months of their early years in the community living in this environment which Father William's vision created, and which his spirit sustains. If we are to be means by which anything valuable is to be achieved and contributed to the experience of the human race, it will best be through discovering, or discovering again after some years, that elusive sense of God's purpose for us, his claim on us which is a claim to be satisfied with nothing less than the knowledge of his loving care, a knowledge which enables us to live in hope, in expectancy, in gratitude, all the more vivid as we know over and over again that it is at the point of our failure and defeat that he returns to us to restore us and start us all over again. This is Father William's gift and heritage to us.

Glasshampton, June 1977   ALBAN S.S.F.

" He was a man of great desires; and it seems that God was so contented with the sight of these pure desires that he allowed very few of them to be satisfied. I see now that to the extent to which immediate realisations were refused to him, to that extent he was acting for the future and not for his actual time—an example of that absolutely mysterious action of an instrument of Divine Causality which breaks through space and time. I can still remember him talking to me of these things as we were walking one evening in front of the cathedral of Versailles outlined in dark splendour in the clear light. ' Jacques ', he said, ' the fact that a work is quite evidently useful for the good of souls is not sufficient reason for us to rush to carry it out. . . . God has his own time. It must first be desired and be enriched and purified by that desire. It will be divine at this cost. And the man who will be charged with carrying it out will not perhaps be the one who has best understood it. We should beware of a human success that is too complete and too striking; it may conceal a curse. Let us not go faster than God. It is our emptiness and our thirst that He needs, not our plenitude '."—JACQUES MARITAIN on P. Humbert de Clerissac, O.P. (From preface to *The Mystery of the Church*.)

PROLOGUE

NEAR the village of Astley in Worcestershire there lies, wondrously hidden away in rolling pasture-land, a beautiful park notable for its gracious views, its fine trees and richly wooded glades. It seems to have been once the property of Benedictine monks, but few if any traces of their tenure remain. Even the manor house of later centuries—a mansion of fabulous splendour which, before its destruction by fire, used to dominate the district—has vanished so completely that its site can scarcely be discovered. Its fine gardens, beautiful chain of lakes and magnificent stables alone survived its destruction. But a monastery there is today, near to where the big house stood—the creation of one man, who, believing he was called by God to live the life of a monk, found here in the disused stable the place intended for him, and transformed it into a Religious House. He did not live to see its cells filled by men like-minded to himself; yet he died in hope and faith that such men would come, men who, called by God to the Religious Life, would have the same conviction as he himself had held: that the primary claim of God was not for their activities, but for the hallowing of His Name in worship and prayer and in the hidden life of contemplatives.

By faithfulness to this call, such lives will in countless ways glorify God, give a supreme witness lacking in our Communion to the truth of the Faith, and have power thereby to win the salvation of souls and to strengthen the active orders and ministry of the Church in their fight against sin and in their efforts to alleviate every kind of misery. But these indirect fruits of their life will flourish in proportion as their life is set wholly *Godward*. Hidden with Christ in God, they will seek no other end but that which is the essential goal of the whole created world, of the human race in particular, and of the Church above all—His perfect adoration in spirit and in truth, that God may be All in All.

Father William, friar, monk and solitary, was the creator of this monastery of St. Mary at the Cross, Glasshampton. His character and friendship are for very many souls among the most sacred of

memories.   The witness of his life—both achievement and failure
—seems to some to hold a word of God that is of signal importance
to our generation.   It is a word relevant both to the Church
and to the world.   It has its significance for those whose mind
is set on a new social order, the evangelisation of the masses,
or on the reunion of Christendom, as well as for those whose
special interest is the history and development of the Religious
Life.   But the man of whom we write was at once so comprehensive and so simple that his life strikes a deeper level than any of
these particular quests, with all of which it is associated.

It is the life of a late starter—one who, after doing fine work of
other kinds, was already a priest of tried talent and distinguished
reputation when he found himself, on the threshold of middle-
age, recreated for a new and simpler work for God, a new life
in Him.   It is the life of an early starter—one deprived of educational privileges and thrown into the world to fend for himself
at an early age, yet showing from the very beginning the strength,
beauty and diversity of the heritage of a Christian Englishman.
And most specially is it the life of one who never ceased to go
forward.   He was growing in grace and wisdom to the end.

Some friends of his have done their best to weave together
memories of this faithful, much-tried, most enlivening and uni-
versally beloved servant of Christ.   Intercourse with him was
to hundreds a life-giving benediction communicated in ways
too intimate to admit its being here recorded.   Every type of
these—the young men and women with the world before them,
the broken and prodigal souls, young priests and aspirants to the
priesthood or to the Religious Life, experienced Government
servants, artists, schoolboys, dock-labourers and country folk,
lepers and other such sufferers, Franciscans, Benedictines,
solitaries, most of all, perhaps, ordinary professional or domestic-
ated men and women—all felt that Father William belonged
specially to them.   And so it was and is, though some of these
types are more inclusive than others, and hold within themselves
the secret of the others.   What sad inadequacies there are in our
portrait of so rich a spirit!   About much, silence has been delib-
erate, as he would have desired.   It has been said he would have
resented any record of his life, and that lives hidden with Christ
are to be *kept* hidden.   But this sketch has been widely demanded,
not only by his friends, and not only by members of his own
Church and nation.   And does not nature sometimes leave

exposed the roots of an oak so that the depth and strength and complexity of its foundations may be visible? And does this not give wholesome, and sometimes timely warning to a woodman as to how to plant and how to abstain from planting? Here maybe it was a special providence that has made visible the roots for the sake of those who follow. For William belongs most of all to a race that is even now being born through the travail pangs of a dying world. Events of today *underline* the challenge that his life presents. It was at the close of the 1914–1918 War, after keeping vigil through those four years, that he was set free to undertake his great task. Others are now awaiting the opportunity of setting out along the same road. They will profit by his experience and avoid his mistakes. At the same time, this life gives to a wider Christian public the opportunity of having a more vivid glimpse than is ordinarily possible into the work of certain types of Christian discipleship, their harmonious interrelation and the tension between them.

And for every kind of reader there is William himself, Friar, Monk, Solitary and Guide of souls. May what he is—above all, his silence—find utterance for each in these pages. For despite the defects in this portrait and in the man himself, you will as you read find yourself in the presence of one who was and is a blessing to the whole world, because he learnt to live—and lives—in God.

PART I

THE MAKING OF A PRIEST

I

BOYHOOD

Blessedness and holiness and sacredness are bound together in one. But of these three, be certain that sacredness is your chief business.

H. BELLOC, *Portrait of a Child.*

WILLIAM'S personality was a rich one, not least by reason of inherited endowments—the life both of sea and of soil was in his blood, and he was indebted to the traditions, military and religious, of the French and Irish strains from which he sprang. He was not an Irishman, though often so described. His father, Charles Sirr, belonged to a family Huguenot by extraction, Irish by naturalization, which had in the previous century in the history of that country won a distinguished name in the service of the Government. But his mother, Louisa Rix, was English of the English, of wholesome East Anglian yeoman stock, and the un-selfishness and kindliness of her homely character seem to have been from the first reflected in her son.

There was a close and intimate bond between mother and son which held unbroken until her death, and it was from her Norfolk forbears that he inherited his love of country lore and life, his sympathy with labouring men, his love of the poor and his great business capacity. Her father had been at one time captain of a merchant ship; he had left the sea and taken to farming, but for this he had no aptitude, and the care of the farm, with all it involved, was left to his wife and daughter. After her parents' death Louisa Rix went to live with an aunt in London. There in 1859 she met and married Charles Sirr.

Charles Sirr was a good deal older than his wife, and had already had some twenty years of experience in Government service abroad. After graduating at Trinity College, Dublin, in which city his father and grandfather had held the post of Town Major (head of the police), Charles was admitted to Lincoln's

Inn. He became Secretary of the Anglo-Portuguese Commission (1842–3), British Vice-Consul at Hong-Kong (1843), and subsequently Queen's Advocate for the southern circuit of Ceylon. Unfortunately the climate made it necessary for him to relinquish this work, and he returned to make his home in London. Here he practised as an equity-draughtsman for railways and collieries, held a commission in the Royal Westminster Militia, and wrote and published two useful two-volume works, *China and the Chinese* and *Ceylon and the Cingalese*.

Mr. Sirr and his family lived in Augustus Square, Park Village East. This was in those days a pleasant spot enough in which to make a home for a growing family. Indeed, it all but deserved its name of village before the railway-cuttings impinged upon it, leading to the destruction of its gardens and the advent of grime and noise. The serenity of Augustus Square was seventy years ago disturbed only by the bugle-calls from the Albany Street barracks, the muffin-man's bell and the occasional encroachments of Punch and Judy. There was for children the continual delight of watching the canal (visible from the Sirrs' garden), along which passed coloured Dutch barges laden with hay and towed by a fascinating succession of horses. There were the walks in Regent's Park and all the delights its lake provided. There was the capital itself beyond, entrancing and tremendous, an ocean-whirlpool of life holding a treasury of sights to be one by one explored. And there was in other directions much good country still quite unspoilt and easily accessible.

Not many years after his marriage Mr. Sirr met with a particularly bitter financial reverse. His prospects had been excellent, but a substantial sum of money to which he was entitled was diverted into Chancery, and the hopes of the parents for the education of their three children were not realized. He was a deeply religious man, and one who could sit loosely to material things without allowing the loss of them to embitter his life. He took upon himself the duty of teaching the children elementary subjects and religion, and he went with them when they were old enough to the Catechism class of Canon Burrows at Christ Church, Albany Street.[1] At his death in 1872 the eldest son,

[1] Father William wrote to Charles Hull in 1923:

You must remember my dear Father as a sidesman at Christ Church. My earliest recollection of him is at the time when still in *frocks*, his taking us to Church where we stood in queues before the doors opened in order to get a seat—I often sat on the floor of the gallery.

Harry, was only thirteen years old, William was ten and Louisa nine. The financial situation was such as to make it necessary for the boys to earn their own living as soon as possible, and the only school-days Father William knew were those at the day-school for choir-boys founded by Canon Burrows, and later at a similar school at St. Andrew's, Wells Street.

Though the carefree days of his boyhood were so shortened, the most notable characteristics of Father William, both in school days and afterwards, were his infectious happiness and love of fun—characteristics which were present in all he did. Full of life and activity and humour, he had a great love of country walks, which often took the form of bathing expeditions. In later years he could not imagine a Religious who did not take his cold bath every morning. Always the moving spirit at home, his unique gift of friendship soon made him the centre of various groups of friends; and from the first it was clear that his desire was to work in some way in the service of the Church for the good of boys and men around him. But a boy in a family which knew poverty, and with a mother and sister partly depending on him for support, cannot always choose his own way, and though his spare hours and energies and leading interests were to be more and more absorbed in Church work, it was not until he was thirty-six that the way into the sacred ministry on which he had set his heart was open to him.

During these waiting years he was a Sunday-School teacher, a lay-reader and in charge of the work of a Mission above a small shop in the Cumberland Market. By the time young manhood was over he was filling successfully business positions in the West End and in the City. But however successful he might be in these business positions, his heart was elsewhere fixed—upon the warfare of the Kingdom of God and the care of the outcast and poor men and boys around him.

The Rev. Sidney King sends the following notes :—

My earliest recollections of Father William go back to the time when I was about twelve or so.

I remember how he always " went after the boys " to win them for Christ. He told me of one lad I knew to whom he gave his bicycle in order to win him. I have vivid memories of trying to explain Euclid Books when, at a later date, he was preparing for the entrance Examination into King's College.

What remains with me is his humility, his willingness to

expose his inability to grasp the propositions which a school-boy had long since left behind. My brother will, I hope, set out the work at the Mission in the School Room at Arlington Road, the Sunday School, the Tea, the Visiting, the outdoor procession—especially on Good Friday; the number of those who entered into the priesthood—having matured under his influence.

One word remains to be said about Park Village and the parish of Christ Church, Albany Street, in which it was situated. Here the Catholic revival of Anglican Church life had been for two decades in possession. Canon Burrows (memorable not least for his Catechisms) and Mr. Festing, afterwards Bishop Festing, were devoted priests in its best tradition. The life of the parish had been quickened by its having known what was in fact the rebirth of the Religious Life among Anglicans through the establishment (1845) of Dr. Pusey's first Sisterhood, at 17 Park Village; later on the Sisterhood moved to Osnaburgh Street in the same parish, but the Society was later merged in Lydia Sellon's almost coeval Society of the Holy Trinity, Devonport. Ascot Priory holds the descendants of both Sisterhoods. To the prayers and sacrificial lives of the London Sisters and their Founder, Dr. Pusey,[1] the Sirrs were unknowingly debtors.

---

[1] Dr. Pusey would have approved a mention of his daughter, Lucy, who died on the day of the meeting decisive for forwarding the London foundation. He wrote to Newman that day, " I ventured to give her in charge to pray for us all in the Presence of her Redeemer and if it might be, for those institutions to which she had herself hoped to belong ". Keble had the same thought and wrote to Pusey, " I suppose, such seems to be the mysterious connection between things here and there, that it is impossible to know whether the cause . . . may not be rather promoted (though of course we must not expect to see how) by her departure ".

II

LAY-APOSTOLATE

True devotion is nothing else than the good will by which a man holds himself ready for all that concerns the worship, honour and good pleasure of God.
BLOSIUS, *A Brief Rule.*

IN 1878 Father William became secretary to Professor Aitchison, Professor of Architecture at the Slade School. He had already worked in the office of two well-known architects, Street & Cockerell. This had given him the opportunity to develop his love of the beautiful and to train himself in craftsmanship and design. And he had a real gift for and love of painting in water-colour.

While with Street & Cockerell, William, through his lovable ways and unfailing cheerfulness, endeared himself to everyone he met. Mr. Street is remembered to have remarked on the notable happiness of his young clerk's face, undiminished by occasional " wiggings " for what looked like neglect and forget-fulness over drawings and plans which ought to have been de-livered and were not. His employer would hardly have wondered at this if he had known how great was his young clerk's responsi-bility in St. Bede's Mission, Park Street, to which he hurriedly bicycled when the hard day's work in the office was over.

It was on the death of Mr. Cockerell that he became secretary to Professor Aitchison. Aitchison was then building the Arab Hall at Leighton House. He and his secretary became great friends. The work opened up to the young man the riches of Arabian art, as well as countless other avenues of architectural interest. Upon his election to the Royal Academy, Aitchison entertained his staff to dinner at Richmond. The party evolved into a river trip (it might well do so with William there!). The unfortunate host fell in, and William had to fish him out. But, so far from the incident upsetting his spirits, Aitchison insisted on walking home to Harley Street, and on the way knocking up Alma Tadema in the small hours of the morning at his house in Kensington.

Later, when Professor Aitchison gave his Royal Academy

lectures, it was William's work to go in advance to arrange the illustrations. The men who worked for Professor Aitchison found his young assistant the life and soul of the office; meanwhile his work at Christ Church, Albany Street, went on steadily. This brought him into touch with a number of young men who later became well known in Church and scholastic life: in particular, Mr. Bevir, afterwards a master of Wellington College, Mr. Collins, later Bishop of Gibraltar, and Mr. Baker King, architect of St. Bede's Mission Church, and his two sons, Herbert and Sidney King. These were lifelong friends, and some of these names will appear in future chapters.

William was already finding that he could hold an audience by his gift of recitation and reading aloud, and that he could win children by teaching not only religion, but singing; he would vary both his reading aloud and his religious teaching by making them sing or by singing to them himself. Yet, greatly though he enjoyed all this work, he was more and more consumed by the longing to " go unto the altar of God ". When he was about nineteen his yearning for ordination led to his going to see the Principal of St. Augustine's, Canterbury, in the hope of being prepared at that college. But lack of funds and regard for his mother's needs compelled him to put aside the thought at that time. Convinced that money to prepare for the priesthood must somehow be earned, he applied for and obtained a comparatively well-paid post as confidential clerk to a wine merchant in Doctors' Commons. When he spoke to Mr. Aitchison of his intention, the architect was much distressed, but ended by saying that " as he had decided to enter the service of Mammon, he was sure that a great future waited him, and he was certain to become Lord Mayor of London ". Ten years later, when Aitchison was designing the interior decoration at Brompton Oratory, a young man in clerical attire called at his house in Harley Street. Both were amused, after a somewhat formal greeting on the older man's part, to discover that he had mistaken his one-time secretary for one of the Oratorian priests.

Doctors' Commons, William's new quarters, was not only convenient for the purposes of mercantile shipping, it was also near St. Paul's Cathedral. Both were full of interest to this new recruit to the wine-and-spirit trade. He was not seated all day at his office desk: his work often took him down to the cellars in Godliman Street, where he set himself to make friends with other employees. One of these, whom we shall meet again as Cellarer at Buckingham Palace, became a lifelong friend. He would take these men down the Thames for evening or nocturnal bathing-parties—parties vividly remembered after the lapse of many years.

He was sometimes sent to collect outstanding debts for the firm, penetrating many strongholds of worldly life, including Brighton's fashionable hotels. It was, for a young man of his gifts, a unique opportunity for acquiring knowledge of men and manners. He was noting character, taking in everything in his newly oriented world, cultivating varied friendships that were at all times richly offered to him, and enlarging generally the horizon of his mind. In his own firm he was beloved as the best of companions, and respected as much as he was loved. There was always not only that swift recognition of the best in others which made at once for confidence, but something reserved and august which inspired reverence.

During the eight years that Father William worked for the wine merchant in the City, the work for Christ Church, Albany Street, continued strenuously; he was gaining a deeper knowledge of the Faith and the power to express it in face of the problems of the age.

It was at this time he made his first confession to Canon Knox Little, and soon afterwards he came to sit at the feet of Father Benson of Cowley, who was to have a decisive influence on his life.

As a member of the Christian Social Union, in whose open-air meetings, held at the top of Park Street, he was taking part at this time, he met Father Charles Marson, a leader with a vision of the meaning of Christian justice which spoke to his own deepest convictions. He was also intimate with many priests, especially Canon Burrows, Canon Festing, later Bishop of St. Albans, Father Collins, later Bishop of Gibraltar, and Father Hollings of Cowley. But he always felt there was a certain gap in the social application of the Catholic Faith to the needs of the poor, and this disturbed a conscience intimately acquainted with their problems. His sense that the apostolic urgency of the mission of Christ is lost in the network of the Establishment grew ever stronger up to his death. It was not long before his death that he protested to the doyen of the Conservative Party, Lord Baldwin, who was visiting him at Glasshampton, " I have been a Bolshevik *all my life* ". Yet at no moment in his life did Father William falter in his conviction that in the Church of Christ, and in His Church alone, lay the remedy for the social as well as the spiritual sicknesses of our age, and that in God's providence the fullness of the Catholic Faith had been preserved in the Church of England; and that this Church, through her divine ministry of Word and Sacrament, could be the means of bestowing His abundant Life upon society as well as upon her individual children.

After eight years patient work for his firm, William's own savings and the kindness of friends enabled him to resign his appointment and to be admitted as a student of King's College, London. Mr. Sparrow Simpson, who had lately become the vicar of St. Mark's, Regent's Park, invited him to live with him, and he continued his evangelistic work at a mission in this parish of which he was placed in charge.

After a farewell river-picnic for his office colleagues and cellar friends, at which he broke to them the perplexing news of his intentions, the City as such knew him no more.

Canon Herbert King, now rector of Holt, Norfolk (one of the two brothers whom, with their father, Mr. Baker King, we have met already) contributes these memories:

> My earliest recollection of Father William is of meeting him at Mr. Sparrow Simpson's Bible Class for men at the Clergy House, Christ Church, Albany Street. Father William, with his warm, impetuous initiative, dragged me out of my shy silence and retirement by showing a lively interest in me.
>
> He was indeed a quaint unconventional little figure. He wore a semi-clerical hat and a turned-down collar with a white tie. When he went to meet the clients of the wine-merchant his dress left no doubt that he was no man of the world, but both a layman and a man of God: he was anything but conventionally clerical, with his merry humour and good-natured smiles.
>
> Later on, when Mr. Sparrow Simpson became vicar of St. Mark's, Regent's Park, we followed the leader, to whom we were devoted. William Sirr was placed in charge of a Mission in Arlington Road, and there he gathered round him a number of young men who taught in the Sunday School; several of these, beside myself, were ultimately ordained.
>
> The Mission was held in a schoolroom. In the afternoon after Sunday School, we all had tea together, and later he led us out into the streets with Cross and banner and

choir of boys and men in cassock and surplice. We sang as we made our procession, stopping at convenient places for addresses. Then back into the schoolroom, where we had Evensong of a missionary type and he preached. His preaching was neither eloquent nor forceful, but people always listened to one who spoke so simply and was so evidently sincere and earnest.

Visiting from house to house was, of course, part of Father William's method; but sometimes he would walk down the road speaking to everyone he met and inviting them to the Mission. Once, to gain entry into a house, he knocked at a door and said, " May I wash my hands at your sink? " He made many friends at the Mission, among them one who had relatives—agricultural labourers—in Suffolk. By their invitation he and I and another went and stayed with them for a fortnight, sleeping three in a bed and sharing their food and their life. This was a holiday, and I do not think we paid excessive attention to devotions on weekdays—but just enjoyed ourselves chiefly with a small sailing-boat and some minor adventures. He was a splendid companion, able to enjoy what came his way, but single-minded—he never left any doubt about the supremacy of religion in his life. At that time he smoked, though later he tried to give up the habit by dropping pipe and tobacco down an area. But it generally ended in his buying a fresh one a few days later until he succeeded in breaking the habit.

In 1893 we lived together in the vicarage of Mr. Sparrow Simpson, and I tried to help him with his Latin, which I found a desperately difficult task, and I had finally to leave it to others who could give more time. He came back from an examination in the first book of the *Æneid* and said he could not translate any of it, and that he had written on the top of his paper that he had not had time to read more than the first half, and all the questions were on the second half; as he could not translate these, he would write out the translation of the first twenty lines.

He had the greatest difficulty in passing any examination; his leaving school at such an early age and his absorption for so many years in the work of the Mission and in his friends the poor left him little time for study. Yet he managed to pass and to be ordained deacon. But his priest's examination remained. His deacon's year at St. Mark's, Camden Town, was not a happy one, for various reasons—not least the priest's examination looming ahead.

Mr. King remembers visiting him one day at the vicarage

and finding that he was just recovering from the blow given him by the arrival of the news of his failure to pass the examination. He records Father William's avowal (often renewed in later years for the encouragement of sinners) that upon hearing the news he had given way to loss of temper and bad language. This failure he never ceased to regard as a grave dishonour— the gravest lapse in his life. Recovering self-control, he found himself ready to accept the examiners' decision as an indication that he was not meant to be a priest. But wishing to know if there was anything more he could do, he wrote to the Bishop of London to inquire whether any information as to the nature of his failure could be given; he expressed his readiness to accept the verdict of the Bishop's examiners, but added that he felt it might be helpful in after life for one who had devoted his whole heart and mind to preparation for the office of a priest to know how and where he had failed. Meanwhile an admirer, a fellow-student, had, unknown to Father William, written to the Bishop's chaplain to say that to debar such a man from the priesthood would mean grievous loss to the Church. This friendly and courageous act of a very junior priest deserves recording, and may have had its effect, though the Bishop himself doubtless made further inquiries.

To Father William's extreme astonishment, he received in reply to his letter one from the Bishop's chaplain asking him to attend the next examination on such and such a date. This time all went well, though once again all seemed hopeless to the examinee. After the examination he went straight to see the young priest friend above mentioned, Mr. Esau, who happened to be serving a parish adjacent to Camden Town.

" Well, how did you get on? " he asked.

" Everything went out of my head," replied William, passing his hand wearily across his forehead; " it's all up! "

" You wait and see! " was his friend's reply.

Mr. King pays tribute to the Bishop. " There are men," he writes, " like the saintly Curé d'Ars, who was the despair of tutors and examiners and for whom Latin was a nightmare: they have no capacity to become learned theologians, but have the rarer and more precious gifts for dealing with souls. As the French authorities overlooked the intellectual deficiencies of Monsieur Vianney and ordained him, so Bishop Creighton had the discernment to see that though William Sirr could never be a great scholar, yet he could serve God and His Church in other ways, and so he ordained the man whom his examiners had been unable to pass."

These reminiscences of earlier years have surprised friends of Father William's maturity, who came to value his intellectual ability as well as his spiritual gifts. The truth is that his parents' lack of means for education and his own wholesale devotion of all surplus time and energy to work for Christ had delayed his mind's development. He was soon to show that over and above pastoral, social and artistic gifts he possessed the intellectual capacity and the administrative and literary talents of his father's family. All this heritage was augmented and perfected by the grace of priesthood. The years of his spiritual maturity were lived in singular docility to the Holy Spirit, four of whose gifts—wisdom, understanding, counsel, knowledge—are pre-eminently gifts of the mind. And their harvest in this realm was bountiful.

The depth of joy and thanksgiving which overwhelmed him when the good news of his success came, suffused his soul to the end. His was from the beginning a thankful, joyous spirit: joyful for the inalienable gift of his creation; joyful for this wondrous world, with its beauty and its treasury of entrancing interests in the realms of nature and character; joyful for the love which increasingly surrounded him; joyful most of all for the knowledge of God and of our Lord Jesus Christ and for all the privileges of sacramental life. But the news that the longed-for gift of priesthood was to be his meant a degree of awe-inspiring joy that only those can realize who have heard Father William speak the words " GOD's priest ". That he, too, should be called to " go unto the altar of God "—he who had so recently been guilty of mistrusting God's call to his soul! No, he had not been mistaken in taking the words *Sacerdos in aeternum* to himself. The great day of ordination he must have approached with a heart full of an awe like that of St. Gregory of Nazianzen:

> I then knowing these things and that no one is worthy of the great God and of the sacrifice and of the High Priest, who has not first offered himself to God a living and holy sacrifice . . . how should I dare to put on the name and habit of a priest before my hands be consecrated by holy works, and my eyes accustomed healthily to behold the creation and to worship the Creator alone . . . before my feet be planted upon the Rock . . . and all my ways

be directed according to God . . . before every member has become a weapon of righteousness, all dead works being cast off, swallowed up of life and giving place to the Spirit?

This was the standard of spiritual perfection he had long set for himself. But his recent trial had opened his eyes to the weakness of his faith and patience. To the thanksgiving and joy there was now added the note of compunction. Through his life as a priest there was to be a sense of abiding contrition for his own personal unworthiness for such an office. It was the source of his deep humility and self-surrender in accepting the over-ruling guidance and Will of God in his life.

III

FIRST YEARS IN THE PRIESTHOOD
Life in a Vauxhall "Model-Dwelling"

> For the gifts and calling of God are without repentance.
> St. Paul to the Romans, xi. 29.

WILLIAM's first work (in the sacred ministry as a deacon in Camden Town) was not a happy time. He could not feel *himself* in the long black coat and tall silk hat which the vicar regarded as *de rigueur*, and one of the King brothers, then a boy, recalls his attempt to explain to him, with that unique mixture of solemnity and fun which was ever his hall-mark, how the priest was a "peculiar person", and that everywhere he went he must dress in such a way that people could recognize his sacred office. Another friend, a priest, remembers being fetched by William in his deacon-year to take a wedding in the absence of the vicar, and his beaming face when he was mistaken for the verger and given a shilling by one of the wedding party.

It was after William's ordination to the priesthood that he entered into the joy of his vocation. Bishop Creighton showed a further proof of his discrimination and confidence by encouraging his transference, immediately after his ordination as priest, to the more congenial sphere of St. Peter's, Vauxhall, where he found not only opportunity for the exercise of his own gifts, but was under the wise guidance of the Rev. Edward Denny, at that time recognized as one of the best and most spiritual parish priests in the Southwark diocese. Mr. Denny had in his parish a branch house of the Sisters of the Holy Name of Malvern, and for the first time, so far as we know, William came into direct contact with the Religious Life. Mr. Denny's own lasting confidence in his young assistant priest's judgment and wisdom is sufficiently indicated by his having made him at his death his executor.

The parish work of St. Peter's, Vauxhall, was divided on the Guild system into spheres of work more or less independent of each other. Father William seems to have had special care of

the Infants' Sunday School, Girls' Day School, Temperance
meetings and the care of one of the five meetings for mothers—
meetings whose ritual embraced a weekly address, a hymn, tea
and biscuits. It used to be said of Mr. Denny's parish that folk
were " washed into heaven on tea ".

But though the accustomed ritual may have continued, a new
note began to ring out in Father William's handling of it. The
Church of that age had written on its heart the motto, " The
poor shall not always be forgotten ". Here was one of her sons
who resolutely refused to set them over against himself as " the
poor ".

Faith in the Incarnation, as William saw it, involves for a
priest (himself, by reason of his priesthood, an *alter Christus*),
the fullest, the most costingly real entry into the conditions of
those to whom he is sent. His must be a true immersion into the
stuff of their life and the completest possible identification
with them. This conviction was a root-motive of Father William's
ministry and life. His subsequent withdrawal from the world, so
far from indicating its obscuration, was, paradoxically enough,
somehow grounded in this conviction : he proclaimed it no less
compellingly in the desert than he manifested it in London. His
cup brimmed over with joy in his last years, when a priest closely
associated with Glasshampton, not long after taking an apostolic
mission at St. Peter's, Vauxhall, settled down unsalaried in
poor quarters in East London to live out these implications of
the Incarnation.

So now in Vauxhall, as the logic of his faith demanded, with
his vicar's permission gladly accorded, he made his home in one
of the river-side blocks of " model-dwellings " not far from the
south end of Vauxhall Bridge. " Just like one of us : he did his
own cooking, and kept it all so clean ! " was the verdict of one of
the other poor.

His little home was a corner-flat on the ground-floor, with
a door opening to the street upon which loafers and idlers would
come to sit and talk. Their language was sometimes so intolerable
that he would open the door and say, " Now, I don't mind you
sitting here, but I can't have that kind of talk on my doorstep ".

He worked in this parish for a little over two years, but at a
parish party forty years afterwards one would find folk whose
faces brightened at the name of the young priest who had lived as
one of themselves, helping them all the more generously and

capably to bear their burdens since his own load seemed to include some problems and duties of their own.

To the drunkard and the afflicted he was specially drawn, and in one way or another he continued to help some in Vauxhall to the end of his life.

As a parish priest he was greatly loved, both by the staff and people. Full of joy and the love of God, full of fun and the love of His poor, his work stands out as being specially marked by the fruit of the Spirit. His very entrance into a room seemed to bring peace and the presence of God; a presence recognized by all, though William might only be telling stories or reading the *Pickwick Papers* aloud. It was a usual sight to see him outside the church surrounded by a crowd of boys and young men, with whom he was on the best of terms and whom he counted as his truest friends. He was not a great preacher, but the simple earnest teaching of his addresses and Confirmation classes, always full of the love of God, left an indelible impression.

Despite the freedom and happiness of his work under the vicar of St. Peter's, Vauxhall, and though he had very largely escaped from those social conventions which had so distressed him at the beginning of his ministry, there was still much in him that was unsatisfied. For instance, while living in the common lodging-house he was receiving a salary as one of the staff of St. Peter's—a salary of which he could not, in his present position, divest himself, and there were other social and economic privileges associated with the office of an Anglican priest which, he felt, separated him from the people. Along with this distress about outward circumstances came the inward trial of spiritual darkness and dryness, the intensity of which even forty years later still stood out in his memory. For months now (he recalled later for the comfort of others similarly tried) there was, as he celebrated the Mass in St. Peter's, " nothing but bricks " before his face.

About this time, as one of the priests in a mission at Southend, the discomfort of his soul reached a climax in the discernment of the need, at least for himself, of apostolic poverty if he was to carry out his ministry. He went back from the mission with his interior questioning unsatisfied. Shortly after this mission he went into Retreat, during which God kindled in his heart an absorbing desire and readiness to do His Will, without light as to what that Will might be.

Returning to his room in the common lodging-house, he found

among his letters a pamphlet describing how two priests, inspired by a novel of Father Adderley,[1] had joined with him to form the brotherhood afterwards known as the Society of the Divine Compassion. He knelt down then and there and wrote to the Superior asking whether he might test his vocation to their Society. He went as a postulant to this Franciscan family in March 1902, after two years work at St. Peter's. Speaking of this time, he would say that he had been forty years in the wilderness before he entered the promised land of the religious life, where he was to find, both as friar and as monk, his true vocation.

[1] *Stephen Remark*, by the Rev. the Hon. James Adderley.

PART II

FRIAR

IV

VOCATION TO THE RELIGIOUS LIFE

SOCIETY OF THE DIVINE COMPASSION

A " religious vocation " if it is real must be an attraction to a life, not a work. The truest vocation would be best described as *a supernatural attraction to the Cross*.
W. in *A Franciscan Revival*.

THE Society of the Divine Compassion was founded by Father Adderley, Father Andrew and Father Chappel in 1894. Its name gives to the world that which was the foundation of the Society, and which has ever remained its purpose—our Lord's compassion for the outcast and the fallen. No one could be too sunk in misery or sin for the members of S.D.C. to offer their ministry. They carried hope, repentance and healing to the broken-hearted whenever they found them.

Through the Society of the Divine Compassion St. Francis of Assisi found his way into the Church of England, where he is ever increasingly at home. The Fathers and their Brothers were, of course, Franciscan Friars, and they showed the way and gave inspiration to those other Religious Societies of Franciscans and Poor Clares who now have their home with us.

When Father William offered himself to the Society, the Friars, priests and lay, had been at work for nearly ten years in those monotonous and unlovely streets known as Plaistow, lying back from the main thoroughfares of the East End in the district of London-over-the-Border. The Friars at their church and mission house of St. Philip had created a veritable oasis of spiritual and material beauty and holiness, and a centre for a sociological experiment of great interest, looking forward to a revival of mediæval crafts and Guilds. They are still there carrying on their blessed work.

17

Though the Society had been ten years at work in Plaistow, and its main lines so well laid down, its interior organization was still in process of development. The first profession of two Brothers had taken place in 1899 at St. Pancras Church, five years after its inception. The professions were received by the Bishop of St. Albans, Bishop Festing, who had ordained one of these Brethren to the priesthood—the first since the Reformation to be ordained in a Religious Habit by a Bishop of the Church of England.

From *A Franciscan Revival*,[1] we take the following Memorial of the Society:

Intercession for all Men.

Ant. Who is a God like unto Thee that pardoneth iniquity?
℣. He will turn again.
℞. He will have compassion upon us.

O LORD GOD ETERNAL TRINITY, look down in Thy mercy upon all men for whom our Redeemer died, and hear our prayers as we bring to the remembrance of Thy Divine Compassion, the darkness of the heathen, the helplessness of the weak, the hardness of the impenitent, the sorrows of the suffering, the self-destruction of the wicked; and grant that the zeal of the Church may be quickened and that all men may come to the knowledge of Thy Saving Name through Jesus Christ our Lord to whom with Thee, O Father and Thee, O Holy Ghost, be all honour and glory for ever. Amen.

Within this glorious supplication Father William was to pass as a living burnt sacrifice and offering of himself to God. In an anonymous article in the same book—one which, I am told, may be attributed to Father William himself—we find the following:

The life of S.D.C. is a humble effort to imitate the Incarnate Life of our Divine Lord. It has its parish work, where it lives a neighbourly life, going out to the more active work of the ministry in preaching and missions; its workshops among the people, where it repairs clocks and watches, works its printing-presses, decorates Churches. . . . It has had, in common with all Christians, its hours of darkness and temptation. It seeks to live a poor life, sharing the privation and discomfort of ordinary poor people. It desires to obey the Lord Jesus in all sincerity and humility.

[1] *A Franciscan Revival*, edited by Clifton Kelway, 1908, Chapter V, p. 2. The anonymous article in question is, it is now ascertained, by Father Andrew. Futher reference is made to this article on page 32.

Important changes were to take place in the Society after his profession, but at the moment when he offered himself its members were fully occupied in ministering to the stricken people of the East End, who were devastated by an outbreak of smallpox at the end of 1901 and through 1902. The Fathers and Brothers of S.D.C. took their full share with the clergy of the neighbourhood in the heroic work of ministering to the sick and dying; at one time there were four hundred victims lying ill at the Isolation Hospital at Dagenham. A Brother recalls his regular visits with Father William, taking loads of parcels on a donkey lent by a friend of the Society. For such work Father William had special gifts: compassion in the full sense of relieving suffering by sharing in it; the gift of seeing the humorous side of things—a gift specially dear to the East-Ender; common-sense, which his diverse experience in the past had enriched, and fear-lessness in danger, which characterized him all his life.

Meanwhile the work of the parish of St. Philip's claimed his devotion, and he gave himself to it unsparingly. He was put in charge of the music, and began the daily singing of Evensong. He chose the music so that the people themselves could sing everything—hymns, Creed, Canticles and Psalms. Years later it still bore the impress of his method. " Most people who have been to St. Philip's ", wrote Father Tribe, S.S.M., " will agree that the singing is here more helpful to worship than in the average church where organist and choir monopolise the music. It is an illuminating fact that the churches which get good congregations of men are those where they can easily join in the singing."

The Superior of S.D.C. at once noted Father William's power with working-men, and gave him a free hand. He began weekly gatherings called " Thoughts for Thinking Men ". The men met in the " crypt "—i.e., the room under the workshop—from 8 to 10 each Monday evening. Some subject, not necessarily religious, was introduced by Father William or another speaker, and then followed a discussion under his wise and able chairman-ship. This was soon a great feature of the work of St. Philip's. Two years later Father Chappell writes:

It has been instrumental in bringing the men to love God. Certainly the number of men who attend Church has increased, and that is specially true of the old men, on whom Father William has a particular influence.

And again in 1906:

The meetings called " Thoughts for Thinking Men " which Father William started are quite admirable. We meet and we discuss. I do not know that many people alter their opinions. It is rather characteristic of the East End of London not to. We discuss every sort of subject, from phrenology to evolution, and from manners to the right-to-work. We go on from 8 to 10 each Monday night, and indeed it needs a stern chairman very often to veto further discussion at the latter hour.

Father William's interest in the dock-labourers found particular outlet in these meetings, Monday after Monday, winter and summer, for nearly a dozen years. Dom Fabian Pole, at that time a Novice of S.D.C., now a monk of Downside Abbey, recalls how the large, ugly, tin-roofed parish hall to which the meetings had been transferred would week after week be crammed with men:

Sometimes it was an outside speaker, at other times Father William himself or one of the Society, sometimes an open debate among the men themselves. When the first speaker had finished, cups of coffee would be passed round, the men asking questions and speaking. It was not parochial. There were men from most parts of the dock district. I did not share Father William's socialistic views, being an unregenerate young Tory, but I can testify to the unvarying good humour and courtesy of the socialist docker in the cut and thrust of debate, and his good-humoured readiness to listen to anything said on the other side. And I can remember, too, among many arguments and speeches which were humorously inadequate, some really brilliant docker speakers.

Impulsive, warm-hearted, always a friend, undoubtedly the strongest impression was of Father William's immense affection for *men*. It was so genuine. He understood, valued and saw all the good in the dock-labourers. And they responded. It was not a professional interest. He valued them for themselves, and they knew it. I remember a couple of cases, each of them men of some ability just going to pieces from " lifting the elbow ". He stuck to them through all the disappointments of such cases, got them new positions in the colonies and kept in touch through the years that followed by letters. Nothing, I think, gave him quite so much pleasure, when he was in charge of the Novice-House in the country, as to invite an East-End docker down for a long week-end and to make it a real good time for him.

The first Retreat of the Community which Father William attended was conducted by Father Benson, the Founder of Cowley. Father William was then experiencing torturing doubts as to his vocation. The intensity of his affection for his fellow-Christians, most of all the young, caused him searching heart-questioning as to the reality of his detachment. On revealing his doubt to Father Benson he was told " the doubt was of the devil ". This simple and definite reply was for William a sufficient answer.

The Superior of S.D.C. at this time was Father Henry Chappell, that priest of " Cornish granite " whose wonderful combination of benignity and strength greatly endeared him to his young colleague. His judgment of William Sirr must have coincided with that implied in Father Benson's counsel. Hence the " stability of his devotion as a religious and the maturity of his life and experience led to the decision on the part of his Superior that he should be professed after a short novitiate on October 5, 1903, in the Octave of the Feast of St. Francis " (Father Andrew, S.D.C.).

It is scarcely necessary to say that it was for Father William a day of as joyous and lasting significance as that of his ordination as priest. " For the gifts and calling of God are without re-pentance " (Romans xi, 29). Yet though he had found the promised land, Canaan also contains the wilderness, for in every human life they will be found together.

Ten years later he recalled this day when writing on January 9, 1914, from Bristol to one whom he had guided into the Religious Life:

> Dear Sister Mary Grace,
>   I hear that you are to be professed tomorrow, and I shall have the joy of remembering you at my Mass.
>   I wish I could ask to be present, but, as you see, I am now a long way off. I am sure it will be the happiest of days for you, and you must feel very full of gratitude to God [1] for having led you on and for having given you the Grace of Vocation to the Religious Life.
>   As you look back I daresay you marvel at the loving Providence that has guided and guarded you. It is like a golden thread running all thro' life, and you can say, " He has brought me into His Banqueting House and His banner over me is Love ". And I know, too, how you will

---

[1] Father William always wrote the word God in capital letters.

realize that your Profession is only an incident in the way of His Will—albeit a very blessed and decisive fact. You will know how you are to grow into all your Profession implies. It is like going down into the Valley with our Beloved to gather the little bundle of myrrh—the Valley of humiliation and submission and absolute surrender. As we tread the valley He shews us very beautiful things. We go on to learn more and more of the Truth. Sometimes the things we learn will be painful just because they are true—especially about ourselves. But however far we travel, or however deep the valley, we shall always find He has been there before us and is ever waiting to receive us. We know, too, that it is only out of the experience of the depths of penitence and submission and surrender, and oblation, that there can spring and grow up the spiritual fruits of Love and Joy and Peace.

So, dear Child in our LORD, I pray this happy day will be for you one ever to be remembered as the day you finally and irrevocably sealed the oblation of yourself to our dear LORD and tasted in the truest sense how gracious He is.

GOD indeed ever bless you more and more. . . .

WILLIAM S.D.C.

V

SUPERIOR OF THE SOCIETY

Work Among the Unemployed

A religious will realise his full vocation only in as far as he takes the stamp of his rule.

A Monk of Parkminster.

For fourteen years Father William lived the normal life of a member of the Society of the Divine Compassion. Its ideals were congenial, its ethos natural to him, and these years of his life formed in him the character of a Religious. And there is no doubt that upon the Society itself, to which he owed so much, he left the virile mark of his own personality and gifts: first as novice, then as professed Brother, later in the positions of Novice-Master and Provincial of the South African work, and then as Superior of the Society.

Important changes took place in the life of the Society shortly after Father William's profession, and with some of these his memory is closely linked. In 1905 a house was bought near Stanford-le-Hope, Essex, to serve as a training house for novices, a place of retreat for missionaries and neighbouring clergy, and a house of prayer for those who had grown too infirm for active work. The house, so accessible for Plaistow, yet so secluded in its rural quiet, is still there today, a stronghold of prayer and peace for the Society and its friends.

Attached to the house was a barn, some farm-buildings, pig-styes and a dilapidated stable with ten acres of land. There took place under the hands of Fathers and Brothers a transformation of a similar kind to that which is the glory of the monasticism of the so-called dark ages. In the achievement of this change Father William took a major part.

The old buildings and the wilderness in which they stood provided the occupants of the house with work for the afternoon. The mornings were devoted to Chapel, house work, reading and work in their cells. An orchard was planted; a vegetable garden and poultry-farm cultivated to supply the refectory table; the

23

pig-styes—"blushing with geraniums beyond all recognition"—
became a greenhouse; the garden with its rustic Calvary owes
its creation and its character to Franciscan hands; the house
itself and the old calving-shed were converted into a monastery.
The stable was transformed into a Chapel. The House of the
Divine Compassion at Stanford-le-Hope is eminently worthy of a
reverent visit by lovers of St. Francis.

Father William writes to his brother from Stanford on May 28,
1905:

> We are settling down very happily—five of us—and
> I very much appreciate the glorious quiet and peace of
> this place. The scenery is surprisingly beautiful for derelict
> Essex, the May luxuriant and the birds in full song. I only
> fear I shall wake up presently out of a dream. It seems to
> be too good to be true, and so much more than I deserve.
>
> I am beginning to understand the Religious Life a little.
> I hope to gain much that will help in a more parochial
> sphere later on. As yet we have had our hands very full
> in putting the house in order: staining and beeswaxing all
> the floors etc., besides outside work; draining a filthy
> farm-yard and levelling it up for turf and getting a building
> ready for a future Chapel. So we have no time on our
> hands.
>
> I did the first wash last week; the clothes dried beautifully
> on the grass, and I felt very virtuous. We have had two
> Tilburys and the surrounding Rectors to see us. Someone
> comes from Plaistow every week, and the Superior takes a
> quiet day next Wednesday here.
>
> I am sure you will pray for me sometimes, with my re-
> sponsibilities, which happily are made light by the great
> goodness of the dear brothers.

The previous year Brother John Mark, a member of the
community, had left for work in the Bloemfontein diocese at the
wish of the Bishop, Dr. Chandler, who, when vicar of Poplar,
had been the Society's neighbour and friend.

Brother John Mark, who had studied theology under Dr.
Darwell Stone at Dorchester, was ordained to the sacred ministry
by Bishop Chandler and given charge of St. Mary's College,
Thlotse Heights, Basutoland. To support him from home, two
Brothers were sent out, but the idea of a Branch House, for
which there must be three members of a community, did not
mature, and ultimately Brother John Mark was left alone. He
stayed at St. Mary's College until it was closed by the diocesan

authorities. His recall by his community entailed a break in the missionary work of the Society.

These changes involved Father William in two journeys to South Africa. First in 1905, when he was sent out to be Provincial Superior at Thlotse Heights, and the second time as Superior of the Society at home. Though he did not remain long in South Africa on either occasion, he carried with him in after years a great love for what he recalls as " the witchery of those vast spaces and eloquent silences, the expanse of veldt and sky . . . the romance of tumbling torrent, the majesty of the mountains ". But most of all he loved " the African himself, whose dark face " he had seen " change and light up " with the knowledge and love of God.

On October 4, 1906, he was elected Superior of the Society, an office which he held for six years (he had been Novice-Master for some years previously). His first important step after taking office was to return to South Africa to review the situation at Thlotse Heights.

He landed at Cape Town on December 12, and stayed at the mission house of the Society of St. John the Evangelist. His journey to Thlotse Heights, largely by construction-rail and Cape-cart, was a severe one, and on arrival he was seriously ill with dysentery. After a short stay he returned via Bloemfontein, reaching England in February 1907. He had written to his sister:

17 *December*, 1906. *The Deanery, Bloemfontein.*

Here I am sitting out on the stoep or balcony. It is a magnificent day, all brilliant sunshine—not a cloud to be seen. And yet not excessively hot. The thermometer is 83 in the shade.

I reached here in time for 11 o'clock service yesterday (Sunday), and leave for Modderpoort to see the Bishop tomorrow, and then I go on to Thlotse Heights.

I stayed a night at Cape Town with Father Bull of Cowley, and broke my journey again after two days and nights in the train.

This is a large town of 50,000 inhabitants, including natives, and it is quite a relief to see trees and civilization. I slept one night in a Dutch farm-house about 200 years old. All the way up from Cape Town you see nothing but the veldt and huge hills, mostly rocks—no grass or trees, only a sprinkling of stumpy bush. There are the block-houses and trenches just as the soldiers left them after guarding the telegraph wires, the whole way up. Here and there are the graves of those who were killed. The train travels very slowly. There are bunks—three each side of the compartment.

In the garden here are beautiful flowers. I went with the Dean to see the Governor, Lord Selborne, cut the first sod for the new railway from here to Kimberley. It was a brilliant sight—the ladies with summer clothes and parasols.

I sat in Choir in the Cathedral last night.

I know the Dean—he was at Poplar, St. Nicholas, Blackwall Stairs—and I had preached for him there.

And on December 23 he writes to his mother:

St. Mary's College,
Thlotse Heights.

You can hardly realize what a lovely time I am having. I stayed at Cape Town, Naumpoort, Bloemfontein, Modderpoort and Flicksburg on my way up here. This is a very beautiful place. It took two hours to drive here through most magnificent country from Flicksburg. I was driven by a native in a Cape-cart through the mountains. You come up a very steep mountain to this village. It is over a mile above sea-level. As I came in about 11.30 in the morning it was a lovely day and brilliant sunshine. The earth is a deep red, and the natives are dressed in gaily coloured costumes and riding about on horseback. The trees are very luxuriant, and the little huts of the natives dotted about irregularly made a very pretty picture.

There are beautiful grounds to the College, and the fruit trees are heavily laden with apples, oranges, peaches, mulberries, etc. There is also a medlar tree. It is beautifully cool, though the sun is, of course, very hot, but I have a great big hat and do not feel it at all. We are going to dine at the Residency on Christmas Day.

The sky out here is very deep blue, and the moon makes it as light as the days are in London very often.

I like the natives very much. They are so cheerful and they have such beautiful teeth. . . .

I am feeling in splendid health. I wish you were all here to see the lovely sights and enjoy the charming weather. We are surrounded by a range of most majestic mountains, and there are many splendid flowers.

12 *January*, 1907.

I never appreciated Christmas and Epiphany as I have

done out here. You see how Our LORD attracts all nations to Himself. The natives are very emotional and reverent. It almost brings tears of joy to your eyes to see them in Church when you dimly realize what it means to God.

And to Charles Hull he wrote:

> Just one word. I had a splendid voyage out. Think Africa grand. The grandest part I've seen is Basutoland. Quite beyond words. A great country on the eve of big developments. Held up here through long and heavy rains. Roads frightful. Rivers impassable. Want to get to Sacred Synod and Missionary Conference at Bloemfontein. Shall try today. In love with natives. Most fascinating. Especially the boys. Hope to catch " Africa " at Cape on 28th. But if business is not finished, " Suevic " a month later.
>
> Had a week's dysentery. Frightful. But they say all the better for it.

The winter of Father William's return to England was particularly severe, and the misery of unemployment was rife among the dockers in the East End. No real attempt was made on the part of the State to remedy its hardships, nor was there any sense of the scandalous injustice of the sufferings involved. It needed a prophet to stir the conscience of a Christian nation to a sense of its responsibility for the workless and starving. And in this awakening Father William played a foremost part.

It was on May 14, 1906, that London was first made aware that there were those who, in the name of Christ, demanded that justice should be done to the half-million dockers and others who were in helpless destitution. On the front page of the *Daily Mirror* of Tuesday, May 15, we find the heading: " *Clergy Join the Procession of London's Unemployed* ". This heads the four photographs which fill the front page. Underneath the description runs:

> A procession of workless marched from the Embankment to Hyde Park yesterday. From every direction . . . detachments streamed to the *rendez-vous*. Father William, in the central foreground, led the West Ham and Plaistow men with a banner bearing the words, " *In the name of Christ we claim that all men should have the right to live.*"

Another striking banner is shown in the picture bearing the inscription:

"God and the Church teach that all should work. We ask for work for those who want it."

There is also a view of the assembled men on the Embankment, with Father William in their midst in his friar's habit and cloak.

It is interesting to know how Father William came to be in the foreground of this event. He had written to a friend in Lent of the destitution of the men in Plaistow and of the sufferings endured by them and their families, saying that he felt he could not go through Passiontide without trying to do something for them for Christ's sake. When he heard there was to be a procession of the unemployed to London, he allowed the West Ham organization to know that he would sponsor them if they made their appeal in the spirit and name of Christ. The next morning St. Philip's was crammed to overflowing with men only. They heard Mass, and the text of the short address was: "I will go forth in the strength of the Lord God. I will make mention of Thy righteousness only".[1] Then in habit and sandals, preceded by Cross and banners, Father William went with them at the head of their procession as they streamed forth to take their place among the crowds marching to the Embankment and Hyde Park. All day long they tramped, true to their convictions.

"We must have seemed a weird sight," writes Canon King, himself a participant in this morning demonstration. "I was working with Percy Dearmer at St. Mary's, Primrose Hill, and my colleague, Conrad Noel, and I, in square cap, cassock and gown, joined him on the Thames Embankment, where he had drawn up with Cross and banners: thus in his friar's habit and sandals he led his party, all communicants; an ecclesiastical episode in the midst of a ragged army of about 10,000 unemployed men marching from the Embankment to Hyde Park."

"There is no doubt that this group stirred the public imagination. For more than one newspaper showed Father William's figure as he was then, and his comradeship and championship of their interests have never been forgotten by those whom he shepherded."[2]

The participation of Father William in this demonstration may be regarded as a prophetic gesture to point the message

---

[1] Psalm lxxi. 14.
[2] The substance of this paragraph comes from Father Andrew's obituary notice of Father William in the *Church Times*. To him and to the Rev. Canon H. A. King, rector of Holt, we are indebted for much information.

he was to be called to give to the Church. This finds expression in his pamphlet *Workless and Starving*, issued at one penny, which sold so rapidly that it soon reached a fourth edition. The contents are a red-hot expression of what ought to be the Christian attitude to the problem of the unemployed. Though unemployment insurance has since those days given relief, and latterly, owing to war conditions, unemployment has largely disappeared, we are still in need of learning from Father William how to approach the problem from what is really the only valid point of view—viz., " *All men have as much right to live fully as we have* ".

Would that there were space to reprint the whole of this, or, better still, the anniversary sermon called " The Love of Man " which Father William preached for the Guild of St. Matthew, at St. Mary's, Charing Cross Road.[1] We have here, in simple, glowing words, some of which will be quoted, the conviction of one who simply and whole-heartedly apprehended the Incarnation of the Son of God as the supreme Divine Act by which God expressed in terms we can understand the fullness of His love for man.

This passage from " The Love of Man " contains, at least in the latter half, an unintended self-portrait, as well as a sample of his simple but forcible way of expressing himself.

> The great message of the Incarnation is that GOD came down. He humbled Himself and made Himself of no reputation. He took upon Himself the form of a servant. He was in our midst. He condescended to put Himself on our level as a brother. He came to our side to help us. He shared our sorrows and our shame. He made it possible for us to share the riches of His glory.
>
> The Church is the perpetual expression of all this. Her members have to be true to the spirit of the Incarnation. They must not be haughty. They cannot look down from an eminence upon their fellow-creatures. Pity and mercy are not always virtuous. You must first be sure you are in a right position to be pitiful and merciful. Such virtues cannot be exercised from a false and exalted position. You cannot bestow them as with condescension upon inferiors. You must be as a brother. Any unfair advantage must be laid aside. You must assume no superiority. No one can be beneath you. If you mean to be a Christian, then it must be a real equality. You must come down. You must

---

[1] Also issued in pamphlet form from St. Mary's Press, Plaistow.

have no desire to bolster up your position. You must be in
their midst, ready to share. If need be, everything must go.
You must be willing to part with all for Love's sake. . . .
You cannot keep back part of the price. It must be a
thorough surrender. No shamming will do. You must do
it all, not grudgingly, nor of necessity. GOD loves a cheerful
giver.

Once you grasp this, once you realize the fullness and
completeness of the Incarnation, once you understand your
Religion, once you hear the Master's call " Follow Me ",
you will know there can be no shuffling, you will know it
must be a whole-hearted response. All dishonesty, falsehood,
lying, pride, self-assertion and self-seeking must be shaken
off. All the ill-gotten gain must be delivered up. You
will get no true peace any other way. It is either the
Religion of the Incarnation or it is no religion at all.

Ah, it's a hard saying, who can receive it?

But if you have humbled yourself to the very dust, if
you have drunk deeply of the teaching of the Incarnation,
then you will have the great joy of being able to love your
brother. Then you will be in a position to exercise the
virtue of Charity. Then you may be sympathetic. Then you
may have mercy and pity. Yes, then! but not till then.

" Unfathomable kindliness and personal interest towards
each one of us," was the impression Father William left in
his community during his six years as Superior. His love for
man which gave him this, and what had been called his " unique
power over working men," was rooted in the love of God.

This sacrificial aspect of his pastoral work in Plaistow had as
its background the life of austere recollection and prayer at
Stanford-le-Hope to which he returned at regular intervals.
Memories of these days emphasize especially his accessibility
to his brethren, his strictness in upholding the principles of silence
and enclosure, his vigour and enterprise in the manual work of
the estate, his belief not only in the power of prayer, but of the
activity of the devil. He is remembered also as one whose warm,
impulsive sympathies sometimes resulted in errors of judgement.
But above all he is remembered as a lover of souls and the
exponent of the Incarnation as the Divine act of Love.

VI

CALL TO THE LIFE OF PRAYER

HOMES OF ST. GILES FOR LEPERS

In order to attain the Citadel of Contemplation you must begin by exercising yourself in the field of labour.

ST. GREGORY THE GREAT.

THE six years during which Father William was Superior of S.D.C. were years of great activity and expansion for the Society. In later years he accused himself of having been over-active, and would no doubt have endorsed one criticism of his rule as Superior, that he took on too much work both for himself and for the Society.

He was a great missioner, and in that capacity increased the knowledge of men he had gained in earlier years. As a missioner it was largely the industrial districts he visited: in Newcastle his experience of the distress of certain poor areas and the consequent alienation of the people from the Church led him to go straight to the Bishop, who suggested that the man he wanted was the Mayor. Father William was successful in persuading the Lord Mayor—who was even more taken aback by the visit of Father William in his friar's habit than the Bishop had been—to make a personal appearance at a big meeting in the distressed region of his city.[1] Oxford undergraduates and students of theological colleges for whom he was often a chosen speaker remember his conveying to them along with a vivid impression of his work among the poor, a real sense of the meaning of the Religious Life.

But however engrossed Father William might be in the activities of his Society, he did not lose sight of the primary purpose of the Religious Life as a family of men detached from the world and consecrated to God as the means of bringing them to Christ.

It was to guard this that the Society had formed at Stanford-le-Hope the second House of S.D.C., which was of special value for the training of the novitiate. Again and again in his teaching of those years he emphasized this principle:

[1] As a result of this meeting the Newcastle Housing Scheme was inaugurated.

There are two aspects of the Holy Eucharist: the aspect of *sacrifice* and that of *communion*. In the same way, there will be two sides in the life of a religious: the life of prayer and the life of work. There will be no rivalry between the two: prayer will sanctify work, work will give prayer its practical expression. One brother will peel potatoes with the greater tranquillity because another is praying in the Chapel. One will remain at his prayer because another is out in the active work of the mission. The sacrificial aspect must come first. It is no good to distribute unconsecrated bread to the people; the life must be lifted up before it is given out. In Jacob's vision we are told of the ascending angels first, of the descending angels second.

Indeed, as the years went on he seemed to become more and more convinced of the need of prayer and recollection for himself and those in his care. There are other traces of this in his article in *A Franciscan Revival* published in 1908, from which the above quotation is taken. He was finding that long-drawn-out conflict between the first and second commandments in our Lord's summary of the Law, which is so often for apostolic souls the passage to the contemplative life.

Besides his work as a missioner in the parish of St. Philip's, and among his brethren and fellow-clergy, and as a conductor of retreats for women Religious, he also accepted at this time the appointment as extra-confessor to a community of enclosed contemplative nuns. It was in this work that he became increasingly conscious of the need of priests who were themselves living this life, and later he realised that God was speaking to his own soul.

In a letter written some time after to the Superior of S.D.C. he said:

For a long time past—long before I ceased to be Superior —I had been coming . . . to be conscious of a persistent call to a life of prayer rather than of active work. I did my best to stifle it at first as a temptation, and you will bear me witness that I never shirked any external work and duty— indeed, you blamed me often, and rightly so, for doing more than I ought; but as it was there to be done, I should not have trusted myself or my motives had I not done it.

He also detected in himself a tendency to assume in his brethren a conception of the Religious Life which exceeded the tradition of the community to which he belonged in its emphasis on the primacy of prayer. Hence his longing for the day when God might call him to lay down the office of Superior, so that without neglect of obligations he might give himself more fully to the life to which he was drawn.

On Christmas Day 1911 his beloved mother died. His brother tells how he came to Mass that day at St. Philip's and how aware he was of Father William's great sense of loss and of the warmth of his sympathy. He spoke long afterwards of the consolation that was given to him when a few days after her death he was conscious of his mother coming, just " as in nursery days, to kiss me on the cheek as I lay asleep—the only experience of that sort I ever had," he said.

The coming year, 1912, brought for him the laying down of the office of Superior, and a consequent sense of freedom to live closer to God. He resolved that he would wait and pray for two years, and if he should still find the interior drawing, he would approach his Superior and ask for his release in order to pass to a stricter life of prayer and enclosure.

A Religious of another community who had been allowed to know of his long-cherished desire recalls how, on a visit soon after the Election, he unfastened his cloak, and, the disappearance of the Cross worn by the Superior of S.D.C. being noted, he remarked, " Now I am free! "

The new Superior of S.D.C., Father Andrew, sent Father William to Bristol to open a house of S.D.C. and to assist the vicar of St. Jude's Church by taking charge of the mission work of that parish. The mission house in which he lived and a common lodging-house for men among whom he worked were within very close proximity to a large slaughter-house. This was not one of the least of the mortifications of that time. He gathered men together for weekly meetings as he had done in Plaistow. Though they came, he seemed unable to secure any real response. Religious topics and secular topics alike left them cold and apathetic. Finally one night he went in resolved on a last throw. He said, " Tonight I am going to talk to you about the DEVIL! " At once there was a start of excitement, issuing in eager attention. The scale was turned, and he gained a lasting hold over his hearers.

His second great interest was the Children's Mass. The vicar had entrusted him with the Sunday School: he found it a riot of unthinkable disorder. He proposed a Children's Mass in its place—a daring proposition, not easily sanctioned. Before he left he was full of thanksgiving for these children, for their reverent worship, the quietness of their coming and going and the hush full of love which fell on them in the presence of our Lord.

He had at Bristol the great support of prayer for his work in the first of those Solitaries who were later to be put under his charge, Solitaries whose lives were wholly given to prayer and of whom he was to direct so many in after years. This lady, Miss Butler, lived a life of prayer in a little house in a busy street in Bristol. Her relations were distressed at her life of isolation, for she was delicate and elderly. "What if she should fall ill when there was no one within call?" Father William assured them that God would watch over the end of a life so consecrated to His glory, and it happened as he had said, though long after he had left Bristol.[1]

While he was at Bristol he conducted many Retreats for Religious. His favourite subject was the "Song of Songs". A Retreat on the theme of this Canticle was given by him to the Sisters at Wantage. A letter from Sister Etheldreda of this community gives a vivid picture of Father William at this time: She writes on September 14, 1913:

> We had one of the most beautiful Retreats I have ever been in. . . . It was taken by Father William of Plaistow. I had never heard of him before; a little elderly monk who directly he opened his mouth, you knew he was a Saint. He took the first four verses of the second chapter of the Song of Songs. There wasn't a jarring note the whole time; he was perfectly simple, highly mystical, intensely practical and absolutely free from eccentricity of any kind; on fire with fervour and having a beautiful mind. So you can imagine how lovely it was. I do feel attracted by what I hear of that Plaistow community. Father William is longing to be allowed a plot of ground by the Government on which to build a house for lepers, of whom there are about 400 in England, so that the Fathers can nurse and look after them. So far Government has not consented. I like that kind of religion. Do remember Father William if ever you have a chance of being in Retreat with him.[2]

[1] It was money left by this Solitary who died in 1926, which enabled him to turn the stables at Glasshampton into a monastery. The bequest was made for this purpose only. Father William has sometimes been criticised for the building of a monastery before he had the men by those who did not realise he was not a free agent in the matter.

[2] *The Story of an English Sister* by Ethel Romanes, Longmans, Green & Co., 1918, p. 224. Ethel Romanes was the daughter of the scientist, whose con-

It was during a Retreat for the Sisters of the Holy Name at Malvern that the call came clearest, an interior Voice that would not be silenced, and when the two years' waiting he had set himself were completed, Father William made to his Superior his first intimation of his growing sense of vocation, though he had no interior drawings as to how it could be fulfilled.

There was to follow upon this decision to approach his Superior a four years' ordeal of searching probation which, owing to circumstances, constantly altered its character and conditions. Though engaged through the greater part of this time in the active work of the Society, a conflict of growing poignancy took place within his soul. He had in its beginning two questions to answer. The first was as to the reality and given-ness of his growing conviction, the second as to whether or no he could fulfil what he believed to be God's call within the Society of the Divine Compassion.

It must be confessed that there is much in the years that follow that reminds one of the wooing by Jacob of the daughters of Laban, a story of which monastic tradition gives its own interpretation. Once again in these years we have Jacob giving years of obedient service on the understanding that he is to be rewarded by the gift of the younger daughter—" and they seemed but a few days for the love he had to her "—but once again, as in the case of Jacob, Father William was to find that Rachel, who stands for the life of prayer, was denied him, and Leah, her elder sister, who represents the active life, substituted for his heart's desire.

It must be remembered, however, in this recent representation of the ancient drama that there was a war in progress, and it may be questioned whether, under the pressure of circumstances, Jacob could have been treated otherwise. Secondly, there were in Anglican conditions no precedents for such a departure. In any case, it was the duty of authority to subject his aspirations to careful scrutiny.

Father Andrew, then Superior of S.D.C., after consultation with his Chapter in the spring of 1914, bade Father William go and take part in the work just beginning at East Hanningfield. He was to work there under a rule of enclosure and silence for a year as a test of the reality of his desire to lead a life of prayer. This decision was at first a cause of some perplexity and distress to

---

version as the result of the influence of Bishop Gore was the greatest blow to agnosticism at the beginning of this century.

Father William. For he was doubtful whether conditions at East Hanningfield would afford true possibility for living the life with regard to which he was to be tested. But his growing gift of abandonment to the divine Providence soon enabled him to embrace it with joy. He wrote to a Religious on October 3:

> You will know that all the time I am striving harder than ever just to commit myself to our Lord, while I am full of gratitude for the prospect of soon stripping myself completely to Him in a new way. . . . To some extent it must be right to look ahead. Just now I can see my one need is to keep up my interior soul that I may truly correspond with the quickly happening events; and you know my wickedness and unworthiness. I have been very bold, and perhaps presumptuous, and now it will make a great demand upon me to catch up my life and abandon myself wholly to our dear Lord. I must see to it that I begin at the beginning and skip no lessons because of drudgery or mortification! I want much of that to offer to our Lord, or it won't be a bit real to me.
>
> I have made my promise to GOD that I would ask for nothing and refuse nothing in this waiting time till next October. Now I am conscious that every day that passes brings me nearer my time of release. I am sure I have a great deal to go through in the meantime. I shall go to East Hanningfield with great joy and eagerly embrace all that GOD gives me.

He was certainly right in auguring that he would have a great deal to go through before his release, as the following chapters will show.

Before leaving Bristol for the Homes of St. Giles, East Hanningfield, Father William was sent for his rest time to Helston. He writes on October 28, 1914:

> I preach here twice on Sunday . . . but that helps me, and is no sort of strain.
>
> I don't think I have been very good in prayer. I have simply rested on the rocks in the sun and tried to see GOD behind all this glorious beauty and to let my soul be quiet in that way. I shall go on now to more disciplined prayer for the rest of the time. . . .
>
> I felt Hugh Benson's death very much. It is, of course, very beautiful. But you know I met him at Vauxhall and he came to tea with me in my model-dwellings. I knew the best side of him—that which is revealed in *Richard Raynal*,

Solitary. A man who could write that book alone must have penetrated deeply. . . .

What was the work at East Hanningfield? As Father William had been one of those chiefly responsible for its initiation, it was most fitting that he should be a pioneer in the hard labours involved in actually setting it on foot. It was work for sufferers of a kind whose very existence is refused official acknowledgement in England. He was now to undertake it under Brother Raphael, a lay brother of the Society, as his immediate Superior. His Superior wrote to him:

> I am afraid you must be under Brother Raphael and content with S.D.C. Rule for the present, though you shall have enclosure and much time for silence and prayer. I shall hope to see you very shortly, and then we can talk things over. You have to satisfy the community that your call is a real one and not any deception, and they say, at least the Chapter say, that they are ready to accept the test of your staying in enclosure at Hanningfield as a real test.

Long before this Father William had written to a friend:

> I told you we had been asked to care for some poor lepers. It is likely we shall be able to do this. Friends have guaranteed £600 towards a site and the building of bungalows and Chapel close by here. We shall probably want at least another £500, but I can't say exactly till the site is procured and the plans out. Then we want Trustees that we may merely manage affairs and minister to the poor things. There would be no responsibility.
>
> I wish you would put it all before Father X . . . and ask him for the love of God to help in these ways. I have a letter from Sir Arthur Downes I could send him, showing the pressing need, etc. I think I have really done all I can do now, and must leave it to such friends as I can find to do the rest. Perhaps you could ask Father Adderley too for me. I will write to others also. I think if they could see a leper they could not refuse.

The Leper Settlement at East Hanningfield was the result of negotiations between himself as representing S.D.C., and the Home Office. While visiting among the poor, Father William had found a leper and his wife; the man had been abroad and contracted the disease. They were living in lodgings, but his condition had been discovered, and they were under notice to leave. No one would take them in. After much difficulty

Father William succeeded in persuading some Church folk to do so, and made himself responsible for the man and his wife.

The need of such help was indeed great. It has been calculated that there have been at least one hundred lepers at one time in Great Britain. Yet, owing to the popular horror of the disease, they are not admitted into General Hospitals nor rightly eligible for workhouses, nor knowingly received by private persons into their homes as lodgers. The fear and repulsion they excite may even lead to the refusal to supply them with the necessaries of life. Indignant at the discovery of such cases uncared for, Father William had been amongst those who had sought to urge Government action. The Home Office pointed out that nothing could be done without special legislation, and urged that this would be undesirable, as it would draw to this country alien cases for which their own countries should be responsible. It was promised, however, that no steps would be taken to prevent a private attempt to secure alleviation of their distress.

In 1912 a few friends had met together resolved to take measures to meet this terrible need. During Father William's time in Bristol a little estate with a small house for the use of nurses was secured in a quiet corner of Essex. Here bungalows for the patients were established, and there grew up those blessed Homes for British Lepers named after St. Giles of Provence, the patron Saint of the crippled and afflicted.

The opening of the first bungalow coincided very closely with the opening of the last war. The angels must have contrived it so in obedience to the Omnipotent Wisdom. For there was fierce opposition in East Hanningfield when the facts about the newcomers were made known. For some weeks Mr. Pettit alone of the local tradesmen would serve them with the necessary provisions. But the war itself soon diverted attention, and before very long St. Giles' Homes came to be recognised as the treasure of the neighbourhood.

After arriving at East Hanningfield, Father William writes, on November 5, 1914:

> Well, here I am—I don't think I will tell you very much of others, or my setting, except in so far as these things touch my Rule.
>
> I have a nice little cell and everything that will enable me to do all you wish. I must wait a few days to see how my rules are to hang together. As yet it seems the beginning

and end of the day is right, 6 and 10.   Up to 9.30, when we
say Terce, is filled with Angelus, Lauds and Prime (6.30),
Mass, Thanksgiving and Breakfast, Housework.   I take my
hour's prayer after Terce.   Yesterday I dug till 12.30 (Sext).
Today I am in my cell writing letters.   Yesterday I was
sawing up wood till 4.30, then prayer, Evensong and Vespers.
I go to visit the Lepers and Compline at 9.   I shall be
able to read till 10.   It looks as though it may be wisest
to leave Night Office for the present, tho' I am longing to
begin, and will do so if possible.

The new house is being built very slowly, but I am quite
happy here and I should like to have Harold [1] in these cells
(an old stable) when the House is finished, if S.D.C. will
go in to it and leave me here. . . . We have six Belgians at
Stanford—wounded.   That means they will have a continual flow till the end of the war.   It makes the hands of
S.D.C. very full. . . .

The time will soon slip by, and one will have to be watching
for the place for the new home soon.

9 *November*, 1914.   *East Hanningfield*.

. . . I like *Heliotropium*.   That and the " *Via-Vitae* " on
the Rule of S. Benedict help me much in directing my prayer.
I can see so clearly how it is GOD Himself dealing with me
and giving me a very real novitiate.   As Mother Francis-
Raphael says, " I must suck goodness out of it all. . . ."

I should be very grateful if I might have the Night Office
with a few notes to guide me and fit it in.   We generally
say Compline at 9.   I am trying to get into the way of
reading afterwards.   But it comes rather difficult at first.

We have Vespers at 6 and then tea, and then I wash up.
After that I go in to see the Lepers and read to them.   Yesterday there was a little service in one of their rooms at 11, and
Brother Raphael gave the Address, and another at 5, and I
gave the Address.   The Sisters come to these.

15 *November*, 1914.   *East Hanningfield*.

I have had a very happy week, quite nice and quiet with
plenty to do.   The wood has flown about alarmingly under
my chopping, and my face bears marks of its retaliation !
Sir Montague Pollock and Sir Arthur Downes have both been.
The latter is the M.D. at the Local Government Board who
helped me much in the early days of the Lepers.   The former
has asked me to superintend the planting of trees, as he seems
to imagine I am adept at it through Stanford.   The Archi-

[1] Harold Lloyd, a young layman who had been living a solitary life in the old
Parsonage at Pleshey for two years while waiting to join Father William.

tect, Alfred Waterhouse, has also been, but I did not see him. . . .

I have taken up Chesterton again, and like it in the new light of what you say. And I am plodding through Dr. Inge as best I can in my ignorance of so much that he refers to. I manage to read better after Compline. . . .

I was so glad to see Harold. I will suggest his coming again after I have seen the Father Superior. And then we shall be able to decide about his going to Cowley. . . . Certainly it would not be good for him to be in the life as I am living it now. I don't expect there will be any release from the Captivity until next October, but I can see, more and more, GOD's goodness in bringing me here on the way.

I am reading the " Oddsfish " to one of the Lepers. He is from Mauritius and, I believe, an ex-R.C. He and his wife only want to discuss Christian Science and Theosophy at present, and they are a very long way off and in the mood that resents any overtures, though I do now and then get in something. They are so good.

Later.

It seems almost selfish to be considering one's own affairs with this great war raging, and yet it may mean that GOD means us to look forward and make provision for the effects we may hope the war will leave upon people, in that many will be moved to consecrate themselves to GOD in Holy Religion. That thought suggests that one should go forward faithfully and make one's own contribution.

My own message in Retreat was that I must try to deepen my realization of my vocation as being in intimate fellowship with Our Lord and make a more whole-hearted surrender of myself. Big things are happening in the world's history, and big things are happening in the Church, and therefore big things are happening in one's own life.

We have had a very helpful and beautiful Retreat. Father Maxwell has been strong and good. He was especially so last night on Vocation—how it is different in every life even in the same Community, a personal call into the Sacred Heart of JESUS, not to a Society—only it does not cease, but goes on, and we are to be expectant for its unfolding itself and leading us into new ways. Yet GOD does not contradict Himself, so it is never a call to retrace our steps—to go back and begin again—it always springs and grows out of what has gone before. It is not as though we find He has led us up a turning which leads nowhere and we have to go back and deny the past. He spoke about the sense of loneliness which comes with age, when the life gets uninteresting and monotonous, and of the temptation to seek companionship and ease and softness—especially companionship with the opposite sex—seeking that which we had renounced, which was wrong and sinful. . . .

15 *January*, 1915.

I am sure that this is the very best time of my life. I have never before had such spaces for prayer and recollection, and I can feel I am growing—there is a *filling-in* of that which has come to me with such rapidity in the last two years. It is a finding of myself. There has been a wonderful disappearance of old temptations—those I felt most—but there has been the painful discovery of whole fields of others and of much that I had never thought of. This has created, as it were, new struggles and other conflicts which must go on, and I know I shall take my life-time to make up the lost ground. I have not had so much time for reading as I had hoped to get, but there has been a great deal to do, and I could not feel happy reading, with Brother Raphael doing more than his share of the work.

24 *January*, 1915.

The end of February will bring me nearly to the end of the two years' novitiate. It has been such a wonderful time. . . . If GOD brings me to the opening of the gate at the end of those two years, perhaps I may look forward to being able to shew my deep gratitude.

I want again to tell you of the reality of my time here in the way of opportunities I have never seemed to have before. I believe I shall be able to travel to the place I have felt I ought to attain and yet have never reached. It is indeed a way of interior *battles*, and it is because I am in the very thick of that conflict which makes me think I am at last really travelling. But I know it is of GOD's mercy, and that it has all come about somehow without my choice. It seems I have been taken up and urged along after fifty-three years of stagnation. That is what I meant about the joy—it is the sense that something is happening *within*—hitherto all the happenings have been to a very large extent *without*. There is no great stirring or fervour—no sudden movement. It is all very slow and imperceptible, and therefore it is impossible to tell you of anything in particular. There have been times when I have wrongly sought for ever so tiny a glimpse of the future, but that was impatience and selfishness, and I am sorry. I am quite content to go on as it were swimming against the stream. . . .

5 *February*, 1915.

It is certainly GOD's gift that Father X . . . takes our Retreat in August. My time will be drawing to its close. . . . You were quite right—this year was necessary to me. . . .

You heard the singing of the birds the same morning that I noticed it first. I think GOD will grant you a time of quiet and rest presently. Perhaps the birds are ushering in that for you. . . . There may yet be difficulties in the matter of my moving out of S.D.C. Much depends on my behaviour, but I can see that the Father Superior very rightly will cling very close to me to the end and beyond.

12 *February*, 1915.

I ought to tell you that as the servant has gone and they cannot get another, I offered to do the washing of the Lepers' clothes, and got permission, and started this week. I think I am to clean one of their bungalows also, as the wife of that patient can't kneel. . . . This is quiet work, and seemed to offer a way of self-sacrifice. It will also train me in washing for the new Home.

Whether the washing was too much for him or not, he writes on February 19th:

I find I cannot do what I used to do; it is more exhausting now, and the bones or something are less able to withstand the effort and strain. Yes! the things are disinfected. . . .

You know I began getting up for Night Office Tuesday night. What a real difference it makes—it is another life! It has brought a sense of joy and delight into my life that was not there before.

I have not yet arrived at that realization of the contemplative in prayer that you speak of—the finding of humanity there and the spending of oneself for their sakes in prayer, instead of the old ways of activity. . . .

9 *March*, 1915.

Both your letters came to me in bed. I spoke too rashly when I told you I was so well! I suppose it is Influenza. . . .

The becoming ill after boasting that I was so well reminds me that I must be careful in saying much about one's interior prayer.

The mere reference to it in Confession seems to take the bloom away and I seem to lose what I thought I had gained.

A fuller picture of Father William's life at the Homes of St. Giles can best be given in the words of Sister Clare one of the first to devote herself to this great work in England. For many years after Father William had gone to Glasshampton she was to remain in charge of the Homes. She writes of Father William:

In the work for lepers we started together. We had to face strange beginnings. Nothing at all at East Hanningfield but an old tumbled-down farm-house and buildings and some acreage of pleasant pasture-land. To begin with, the patients lived in the old farm-house with us and the Brothers occupied a row of cowsheds. Even after the tiny S.D.C. Community House was built, Father William joyfully occupied a cowshed, which had become known as The Ark. Boycotted by the neighbourhood, facing all the problems of pioneer work in war-time, in cramped space and with no hope of quick building—such were our problems. But we look back upon that time now as the happiest of all the long years spent at St. Giles. Simplicity, joy and love were there, and we felt we were back in the beginnings of the Franciscan life. Brothers and Sisters met in the beautiful little barn-Chapel for Mass and Office and shared in nursing, housework and spiritual service at the patients' bungalows which gradually sprang up.

To our joy, Father William was sent to us as Chaplain, and gave at once his big-hearted love and service in every detail of our life. His wonderful Meditations and Retreat days were like a sweet fragrance permeating our difficult and often painful work, and as our director and friend he was ever ready with wise counsel to guide us, cheerfully and humbly accepting his share of housework and drudgery. His delightful sense of humour saved many a black day when nerves grew tense and the future looked ominous. Patients and Sisters alike turned to him for courage, and he was able to give a special bit of service to the young lads training in the camps, who spent long Sunday afternoons resting on our lawns, and made a habit of attending Vespers the night before they entrained for the Front.

Pictures rise in my mind. Father William, in a huge sacking apron, curtseying at the Convent door—" Please Mary-Anne has come! "—at a moment when half the Staff were sick and the others " sorry ". Or Father William, discovered by an eminent body of specialists, hanging out the clothes; or digging our hard clay soil, or converting an ancient farm " midden " into a fragrant flower-garden: nothing was too humble or too hard, nothing could cloud his merry smile.

We hear again his tinkling bell as he brought the Blessed Presence to our sick and dying up the long, often bitter, wind-swept path; quiet evening services with the old loved hymns and simple prayers for the aged; placidly reading aloud to the blind while Zeppelins fought above us and searchlights swung and shrapnel crashed in the skies.

He had a wonderful peace-bringing gift to the borderline mental cases we so often had to receive, broken by the horror of their affliction. Perhaps, in work such as ours, his saving sense of humour—betrayed in his twinkling blue eyes—was one of his greatest gifts. . . .

I hardly dare speak of Father William's own vocation and the Gethsemane he passed through when called to leave his beloved community and the life of active service he appeared so fitted for and loved so well. I feel it is holy ground, and only for the sake of his spiritual children dare one lift the veil of his long night-watches in prayer. . . . In the knowledge of his great fight, our souls were raised to fresh courage in our smaller conflicts. He both found peace and gave it to others. Long after he left us, his *Meditations* were in constant use in the community and his letters to his spiritual children were a much-prized gift.

His active life was over, but he left behind the foundations of prayer, well and truly set, without which the leper-work of St. Giles could never have gone on.[1]

[1] The Homes at East Hanningfield are still cared for by Sisters of the original Sisterhood of St. Giles which is now amalgamated with the Community of the Sacred Passion, a community founded by Bishop Weston for work in the Mission to East Africa.

VII

THE YEARS OF VIGIL

There is nothing divine about hurry, no hurry in anything divine.
R. M. BENSON, S.S.J.E.

THE conviction of the need of a life of prayer and reparation in the Church of England and of his own call to such a life had, we have seen, grown upon Father William during his six years as Superior. What could be done? He could not legitimately hope that the community to which he belonged would change its character. Moreover, the Canon law of the Church, while it recognizes in certain conditions the right for a Religious to withdraw to lead a stricter life, expressly forbids a Superior to take any steps to alter his own mode of life while he is in office.[1] As Superior he had been able only to encourage the life of prayer wherever he found it in individuals and communities. His first sentiment on laying down office had been one of joy in his new-won freedom as an ordinary member of an active community to seek how he might now test his growing conviction.

We have spoken of the following two years of waiting and prayer which he devoted to the private testing of his impulse, and have described his pioneer work for the leper settlement. The time spent in retirement at East Hanningfield had exceeded the year which Chapter had decided to accept as a " real test " of his vocation, when a new method of probation was fixed upon.

One can well understand that a religious community which had valued one of its members so highly as to elect him as its Superior for six years could not lightly consider the prospect of his withdrawal, for however great an end. Moreover, it is a commonplace that the devil, who is the father of instability, has designs of special subtlety for the overthrow of the sturdier members of religious communities, whom he often delights to " destroy in the noonday " of middle life. Father William's community was entitled to subject such a proposal from one of its members to stern scrutiny. Its resolution to do so becomes all

[1] See Appendix II.

the more intelligible when one considers the strain imposed upon it by the shortage of man-power due to the war. These considerations explain in some measure the rigour and prolongation of the further vigil that ensued.

It was decided after consultation with the Society of St. John the Evangelist that Father William should go to their house at Oxford to live the enclosed life, and so prove under competent direction his fitness for the venture which he felt impelled to take.

The need of such reference to another community was due to a singularity in the situation of the Anglican Church in its step-by-step restoration of the Religious Life. The recognized principles of the Western Church would have allowed the transference of Father William, after due probation, to an enclosed order for men living a life stricter than that of his original community. But there was at this date no enclosed order for men fully established. Had he realized this call several years earlier, he might have asked his friends the Benedictines of Caldey to receive him. But Caldey had recently been handed over to the Roman Church. A remnant remained true to their Anglican allegiance and was now at Pershore. But the hand that was to guide them to recovery had not yet taken the helm, and to the one priest-monk left the situation there seemed so precarious that he wrote to ask whether he might not have the collaboration and guidance of Father William; this priest shortly afterwards made his submission to the Church of Rome.

The revival of Pershore when it came was not a revival of that aspect of the life of Caldey which most appealed to Father William. For one thing, the enclosure was abandoned. The guiding principle for Abbot Denys was the establishment of the claim to live the Benedictine life within the Church of England, an ideal which seemed to Father William imperfectly to represent his concern for the recovery of the contemplative life. In any case, his *attrait* was always towards the Cistercian[1] rather than a Maurist[2] version of the Benedictine life, and the community whose home is now at Nashdom seemed to him to represent more fully than the tradition it inherited from Caldey demanded, the *teaching* office of the Church.

[1] The Cistercians were Religious of the order of Citeaux, a Benedictine reform established in 1098 with the purpose of restoring through a stricter observance of the Rule of S. Benedict the gravity and simplicity proper to the monastic profession.

[2] The Maurists (1618–1818) were a congregation of Benedictine monks in France, best known for their great services to learning.

As there was then no enclosed brotherhood of men under whose care he could pass to test his vocation, it seemed right that he should make such trial under the direction of a Father of the S.S.J.E. appointed by the Superior, Father Maxwell, who had already been his counsellor in the matter of his vocation before he left Bristol and whose sympathy and encouragement never failed him. This was done, and Father William was placed under the direction of a priest of the Society of St. John the Evangelist, and was at the mission house, Marston Street, Oxford, from November 1915 for fourteen months.

The cause of the decision had been that in the spring of 1915 a cottage with some acres of ground was offered to Father William as a home for himself and others when they were ready to begin community life. This offer was made by the Rev. Hugh Marshall of High Easter near Dunmow, a young invalid priest who through his wife had inherited considerable property in the neighbourhood. They were anxious, for personal reasons, to make some offering of the landed property to God. They knew of Father William's life in S.D.C. and of his hope, and they counted it a great privilege to be allowed to farther it in any way. High Easter, a small parish of a few hundred inhabitants, and about twelve miles from Chelmsford, has a fine parish church, and was eminently suitable in every way.

On May 11, 1915, Father William wrote to his Superior:

> A cottage has been offered me by Mr. Hugh Marshall of High Easter, near Dunmow. May I throw myself upon your generosity and love for permission to go over about it? I feel I may the more easily ask this of you, after what you said last week in Chapter.
>
> Being in my eighth month at Hanningfield, your permission for me to do this would enable me to be ready when the time comes to pass from Hanningfield with my companions and to begin the novitiate without any break or distractions. There is an old windmill as part of the property which could be used for a Chapel, and miles of solitary fields in beautiful country . . . also a second house and room to expand if it was needed.

We do not know whether the permission was granted, but among Father William's papers the following letter has been found. It is included because it gives a careful survey of his position and the difference between the life of a Monk and that of a Franciscan Friar:

18 *May*, 1915.   *East Hanningfield.*

DEAR FATHER SUPERIOR,

     I cannot but know that you have nourished hopes that I might ultimately find my vocation here or in a life of prayer within the Society. May I˙say at once, to clear the ground before us, that I could never find any fulfilment of that life here? I could live a prayerful life here, but that is not all that makes the Monk's life of prayer and penance. Not only does the life here lack many things which make the Cloistered Life, but it is without that which is of the very essence of monasticism—and, as I believe it, even of Holy Religion itself—the complete exclusion of women from the Cloister and its precincts. The fact that those women are or may be Religious (nursing the patients both men and women) does not minimise that evil—it rather aggravates it.

And with regard to the patients, while a Friar rightly goes out to minister to Lepers, a Monk cannot—his life is lived within the Cloister, and it is in the Cloister and its Rule that he fulfils the Monk's Vocation.

It will clear the issues between us if you can know that more firmly rooted even than my vocation itself, is the knowledge that it is not here I am to live it out.

There have been, and there are, many Contemplative Friars: that would not need any change of estate. It is the cloistered life of the stricter monastic Contemplative Orders to which I ask leave to depart, and to which I believe I am free both by the Law of Nature and Grace to pass on, for it is the higher call into the more perfect way that has come to me. I can say that I am unworthy of it—that I am a man of unclean lips—but I cannot say I have not seen the Lord of Hosts, or that He has not made known to me His Will, or that this which you offer me is the way, when He has all through pointed to the Other Way.

I will tell you more. From the first time I went to Father Maxwell he encouraged the hope that GOD's call to me might mean the possibility that through my life GOD might bring forth a more stable Contemplative Community for men in our English Church than we had yet found.

It was not that I sought this. I shrank from it, but he encouraged my desire for the Cistercian life of solitude and silence and manual labour, and there are men, as you know, who desire that life.

Quite unsought the offer of this house at High Easter has come for these men, and I would desire when I leave S.D.C. to associate myself with them.

Is it an unreasonable request, in view of what I have said in the first part of this letter and of the hopes you gave me last September, to ask to see it?

There are points in your letter which make me know that you will see it as I do. You speak of " the claims of the Community to come before that of the individual, and those of the Church before the Community." There can be no greater need of the Church today than the need of such a Contemplative Order for men as I have spoken of. If the call which has come to me necessitates the closing of a House of the Society only to set me free to live alone in quietness and prayer at Hanningfield, then it would not be right to lay such a burden on the rest of its members. If it leads to the beginning of such a Contemplative Life as I have spoken of, then it is the higher good of the Church and of S.D.C. and of every member within it, and must be the means of bringing it into the way of GOD's Will. No act of mine done in obedience to GOD's call can harm S.D.C. or you. . . .

I am not acting in self-will or moving without guidance.

From the letters which follow it is evident that the matter was referred to the Chapter of the Society, and the Chapter accepted Father Andrew's decision that Father William should go to the Society of St. John the Evangelist at Cowley, where he could be more strictly enclosed, and thus test his vocation to the enclosed life. Father Maxwell, the Superior General of the Society of St. John the Evangelist, had already shown great sympathy with Father William's aspirations and approved Father Andrew's proposal.

While waiting for the decision of his community, Father William had written to a friend:

I don't think I doubt about the open door for me to go out. I can see that. But I am timid of renewed argument and controversy. It makes me really ill. . . .

Pray that I may keep gentle and loving and patient. I am sorely tempted to give it all up at times. It brings in so much that is unchristian.

After learning of the decision of S.D.C. he wrote again to the same friend (June 19, 1915):

I saw in my prayer that our Lord is allowing me to go the more difficult way to purge and cleanse me.

It is the way of the Cross—the year here, the great opposition and disapproval of the Brethren—almost the being despised—and then the long six months Retreat at Cowley. I can see it is a beautiful way if I can surrender to it and accept it without any interior rebellion, and I know I shall be the better for it. It ought to make me less restless and managing and conceited—the being here under Brother X . . .,[1] the junior Brother, and then the " burial " at Cowley. Will you pray that I may embrace it lovingly? I can do so if I know of His Presence as I knew it this morning. I am so afraid of answering those letters, for I must be firm, and yet meek and lowly.

The next letter is to Father Andrew, with whom there was always a bond of understanding and sympathy with regard to the inner things of the Spirit:

> 5 *July*, 1915.
>
> I want to try in all ways to remove difficulties. It is to me so open and simple that I can only obey GOD's call. I asked to be released from nothing vital, only from the obligations of the active work of S.D.C. and to embrace those stricter ones of the Contemplative Life.
>
> I cannot be in the new Life as though S.D.C. had never been. I go out of S.D.C., but in a true sense I take it with me. You have taught us that Life. No one will be surprised that some at least should follow it to its legitimate outcome into solitude and silence. Perhaps the surprise is that no one has done so before.

Another close friend in the Society was Brother Raphael, the artist, one of the senior Brothers. He had written to Father William asking him to explain the difference between the gift of contemplative prayer and the enclosed life of a Contemplative Order. Father William replied:

> *July* 19, 1915.
>
> The Gift of Contemplative Prayer, and the enclosed life of a Contemplative Order, are not the same thing. The gift of Contemplative Prayer comes to all sorts of people— men and women, educated and ignorant—and is not confined to Religious as such. For the daughter may have it in the home, or the married man in his family. That is the teaching of the Church, and we have only to read to discover it is true.
>
> It is possible GOD has given you such a gift of prayer, but it would not follow you are called to the Contemplative Life of an Enclosed Order. It would rather point to greater strictness and faithfulness where you are—to refuse to be stuck—but to press on knowing that GOD's Call is ever beckoning forward to a closer union with and knowledge of Himself through the pains of dying to self. As St. Teresa said as a

---

[1] Brother Raphael had been withdrawn from East Hanningfield and a junior Brother put in charge.

child when she ran away to seek martyrdom with a little brother at the hands of the Moors, " I ran away because I wanted to see GOD and I must die first for that "—We all find that in our search for GOD, and that is another dying than at the hands of the Moors.

But to go back—There is that difference between the Life of a Religious House or a life in the world with plenty of time for quiet and prayer, and the life of an Enclosed Order. Just as there is a difference between monasticism and the Friar's Life. The one seeks union with GOD in charity through the sacrifice of the withdrawal from creatures and through the stern discipline of solitude and silence, manual labour and bodily austerity. The other seeks union with GOD through Charity to his fellow-men. The Church has said the former is the higher life. I will not dare to say so. I only know GOD has called me to it, and that I must follow. Both alike may have the gift of Contemplative Prayer, St. Benedict in his cave, St. Francis in his ministry. But both can only find it in obedience to the Will of GOD and in the fiery testing He gives to each. The soul can make no mistake as to His Will.

I must often surely have puzzled S.D.C. in the old days when I ruled it, for, without knowing it, I was always trying to approximate the Society and myself to the ideals of the stricter life. And I sorely puzzled myself too. It was only when I came to see there were two lives, and which of these was my own, that things became clear, and I can have no manner of doubt now, for everything in my life, interiorly and exteriorly, falls into its proper place and there is a unity of purpose as I see GOD's Will in the past and present.

And I am satisfied (in the highest sense of that word)— in GOD. I could not be that, with all that has been and is around me of uncertainty and opposition and the breaking of old ties—which were dearer than life to me—if I had not found the truer meaning of His Will, and mine in obeying it.
With so much love, etc.

The next letter is to a Religious of another community:

August 2, 1915.

I am most grateful for the Novena. I am always fighting with myself in prayer and surrendering all to GOD. Of course it is only that which keeps me, and restrains my impatience and weakness of trust, and as the time goes on *that conflict* is more acute. . . . In theory I know GOD's Will must prevail, but then these doubts as to whether it *is* His Will will come to me, and it is terribly hard to sustain tranquillity and interior peace, so that in practice I dismally fail. Thank GOD I can recognize a certain growth and strengthening somewhere beneath it all, and I think I can see it is good for the future. Yet if I had more love and trust I should be unmoved and full of confidence and joy.

Just after writing the above Father William joined his own Society in Retreat: he writes after it (August 14):

The message our LORD gave me was for a greater surrender and more mortification for love of Him, and He shewed me my resolution. It seemed to come so clearly to me that the new Life is to be *very strict* and *very poor*. Our LORD seems to ask for this quite definitely. There is a wonderful joy coming to me as I realize the privilege of embracing such a life. If we are faithful, such blessings will flow out of it into the life of the Church.

To his own Superior, Father Andrew:

September 11, 1915.

I have been waiting upon GOD and praying. I am more and more clear that GOD is calling me, and though I go out like Abraham, leaving you and the brethren and all whom I love, I *am* going to a land already prepared, and one which He will shew me. There is no uncertainty about it. . . .

I am convinced the Contemplative Life has its place in GOD's revelation, and if in His love He has restored to us in the Church of England the Active Life, He will give the Contemplative Life to uphold it. I know, too, that He has laid hold of my own weak life in some sort of way as His instrument and as a part of something larger than myself; and that my salvation lies in my faithful obedience to His Will. It is this knowledge which helps me more than anything—and will help me in the burdens I shall have to carry.

I know I always have a share of your prayer.

With loving obedience and GOD bless you,

Your ever affectionate

WILLIAM, S.D.C.

It was thus settled that Father William should go to Oxford in the autumn for six months' strict seclusion with the Fathers at Cowley. During this waiting time he was receiving letters from priests and laymen who, knowing him personally and hearing of his purpose, wrote to enquire as to the Life and whether they could join him. There are several notes and answers to such letters, and it is to one of these he refers in the following short letter to a friend:

I have had a letter from a man making enquiries as to whether I was contemplating founding a Carthusian Order. . . . I have replied saying I hoped to live a life of prayer and mortification in solitude and silence with others, but had no sort of plans: I was abiding GOD's guidance. . . .

To the writer himself he says:

Feast of the Guardian Angels (*October* 2).

. . . It is not a fact that I desire the Carthusian Rule. I do not know where that emanates from. What I do desire is to be quiet and learn to pray better, and I am sure that if I am to be faithful to the Vision GOD gives me, I must have solitude, silence and labour. You ask me to tell you my hopes, but it is very difficult to do so in writing, and I can only say quite simply what GOD asks of me; and I believe that if GOD in His love has restored to us the Active Life in the Church of England, He will restore the Contemplative Life too, to take care of it.

Whether He will take hold of my weak life in some strange way and use it to that end, I don't know. But I know the way I have come, and I know if I refused to respond to what He holds out to me now, it would be the great failure of my life. Not only are there the interior leadings, but there are outward manifestations of His Will. From the beginning I have tried to avoid any self-will, and have been guided by my Director, to whom I have made known my life. I shall continue to act under obedience, and whatever I do will be with the approval and sanction of my own Community and, I hope, of S.S.J.E.

After my rest I go to Oxford for an indefinite time to be in retreat and to think and pray. After that I hope to go with others into the cottage at High Easter placed at my disposal, but, as I say, I have no definite plans. I can only be led by GOD, and if there is to be any future of my hopes, they must grow out of the reality of the Life. I think myself the Life would tend to shape itself more on the lines of the Cistercian Rule. In any case, it would not be real, and still less Christian, if it shut out the love of the Brethren and had no share in the sorrows and sufferings of the world. It will be strict and severe. That is all I can say. . . .

Of course, the New Life would be Catholic. The Divine Office in English and the Night Office. Eat no meat and work with our hands. . . .

My position with my own community is that they do not want to get rid of me, neither do I wish to be dispensed or released in that sense. The whole question . . . is as to whether I ought to seek the Higher Life in response to GOD's call, or to stay where I am. The decision that I must respond to GOD's call has been made in the Tribunal of my own conscience under the guidance and consent of my Director. From that decision I cannot go back. What I do ask is the freedom which lies hid in all vows (unless I have expressly put it from me by another vow) to follow GOD's call of Perfection to the end; for me this is to be released from the obligations of active work and Rule in order to embrace those stricter ones of the Contemplative Life to which I cannot but know He asks me to come.

The decision that he should go to Cowley was, if we may venture an opinion, the right one. It was certainly one for which both at the time and in after years Father William was increasingly grateful.

On his arrival there he was provided with gardening tools and a scrubbing-brush, a place at the Guest Table in the Refectory, where he was to have his meals in silence, and the Upper Library to look after. In the old Chapel of the first mission house he was to offer Mass and say the Divine Office night and day in its fullness. He had hoped he would be allowed to have with him, to share his life, some at least of the men who had waited so patiently to join him, but this was refused. It was a great blow, for it meant that his devoted friend Harold Lloyd, who had lived for two years a more or less solitary life, must now join His Majesty's Forces. Very soon the other laymen were scattered too; but as S.S.J.E. had let their own younger Brothers go out to meet the country's need, Father William could not doubt the justice of this decision. So it came about he found himself living the life of a Solitary under the guidance of S.S.J.E.

Father Andrew, Superior of S.D.C., wrote to him:

You are very blessed to be under such splendid direction as you get from Cowley, and I shall consider personally a conformity to such direction a sufficient proof of vocation.

Twenty years later Father Andrew was to write:

In the old Chapel at the top of the first building of that beloved Community where those saints of that great Order— Father Benson, Father Congreve, Father Hollings and others prayed—Father William passed a faithful and searching novitiate.[1]

Father William himself was, as we have said, full of gratitude for the opportunity given him in these months spent in the house and under the spiritual guidance of S.S.J.E. The first springs of his spiritual life as a young man came through its influence. Through Father Benson came his first call to the Religious Life and its strengthening when in a moment of doubt and hesitation as to his fitness for such a life he might have turned back.

In later years when he realized it was not God's Will that he should have spiritual sons in the life he had longed for, and lived so faithfully, he sent to Cowley both priests and laymen who had been with him for a time and in whom he saw the promise of a fruitful vocation.[2] The few letters which remain from this time are full of interest, but after the first few weeks it was understood he should not write to friends. Father William's own letters best convey the character and the meaning for him of this time of vigil. He had a great gift of simplicity of expression, and his correspondents, whoever they were, could be quite sure that what was in his soul came out in his letters. His clear and beautiful handwriting, never hurried, conveyed in a significant way the absolute purity and sincerity of the words he wrote. The following letters show this, as well as the enthusiasm with which he embraced each step forward.

Mission House, Marston St.,
Oxford.

13 *November.*

The old clock arrived this morning, for which please accept my very grateful thanks. No one else seemed to realize I needed it. I have been trying to see which way it " goes ". It seems it won't " go " unless it lies with its face downwards. I may persuade it to act normally as time goes on.

I have never been so happy in my life, and that in spite of the new sense of my utter sinfulness. It is because I am in the way of God's Will for me. I *know* now there is no doubt about my vocation. Oh! that I may be faithful and a wee bit worthy.

If you have not already sent the music-book, may I ask

[1] Obituary notice, *Church Times*, April 2nd, 1937
[2] The only photograph other than those of S.D.C. brethren to be found at Glasshampton was that of the Founder of S.S.J.E., Father Benson.

you to lend me *Holy Wisdom* again? There are hundreds— no, thousands—of books here, and I might easily get away from what will help me most, and I *must* read. How beautiful Hilton's *Scale of Perfection* is and the *Interior Castle*. Of course, any one of those books is sufficient alone, and one might spend all one's time with either, but it is good to know one's way about them all, I suppose, and then keep to *Holy Wisdom*.

Saudreau's *Degrees of the Spiritual Life* and Scaramelli's *Directorium Asceticum* are here of course. The former is best, and is based upon the *Interior Castle*. The latter is very verbose, and full of anecdotes. But both are well worth reading. I have gleaned some help as to the Discipline.

I see the right order in which to read the mystics is English, Spanish, *then* Teutonic.

I came across this by St. Gregory the Great: " In order to attain the Citadel of Contemplation you must begin by *exercising yourself in the field of labour* ".

20 *November*, 1915.

Though I welcome the time here, I can't help ticking off the days. I have been doing that for some years now.

I am in charge of the Upper Library in the New House. Father Congreve lives there. He is very weak, and his last illness has broken him a good deal. It is interesting to notice his books as I dust them. He lives on Father Baker, apparently. He helped Miss Comper of Hampden to bring out her " Richard Rolle of Hampole ", so he has his copy of that.

Also the *Pilgrim's Progress*. I hear he reads this to the lay-brothers. He reads beautifully.

I sit at the High Table for dinner and tea on Sundays, and go to Recreation with the Fathers.

I came across this in St. Peter of Alcantara. " It seems to me that anything less than an hour to two hours is a short time for mental prayer." I think I agree. He goes on to say: " It very often takes more than half-an-hour to tune the viol and calm the imagination." Again, " Possibly the time may be shorter in the morning, because of all times this is the time when we are most prepared for it ". I expect it becomes a matter for the individual to decide. Capacity varies so.

I daresay you have *A Golden Treatise of Mental Prayer* by St. Peter of Alcantara, translated and edited by Father Hollings.

The clock goes splendidly now, and in the right position, too. I wish I could send you a sketch of the Chapel at the top of the old Mission House. I may try to some day. It is particularly appropriate up there over Oxford at the Night Office. It was a bold thing to do. It is all planned so ingeniously. No room wasted.

It becomes very difficult for me to pray. I don't know why. But I am going to be patient. I think Father Baker will help. He always seems to send you away with a greater desire—a hunger—for GOD.

I thought I might use the *Spiritual Exercises* of St. Ignatius in Advent. Is that madness, I wonder? I know I have to go back and review my life and bring my sins again to my Lord. I think " The Spiritual Exercises " would answer a need I seem to feel now.

I am beginning to wonder at myself for daring to be anything. I need your prayers, that I may at any rate be heroically strict and really embrace the Cross. It is a fierce struggle, and I can only reach the whereabouts of my ideal through GOD's grace enabling me to do violence to myself— the old Adam.

3 December, 1915.

I *am* being purged and purified, and I am yearning to be so, still more—that is how St. Ignatius' Exercises came before me. I don't want to shirk or miss anything. I only want to be a good penitent and at GOD's disposal. There is nothing to hinder that. I am free to let go everything and give myself utterly to GOD.

The difficulties I have referred to are there *because* it is well with me. I will not let it be easy.

I have had to kneel out in the middle of the Chapel away from the seats and desks. That is the sort of struggle I have had with the body and sleepiness. It is good to battle through that into reality. Well, it is GOD's love and mercy helping me. He led me out like this to save me from myself.

I shall be all right, I am in GOD's hands. I can realize it more and more now. If there is no one to come and join me in May, then I must be a Hermit—that is all. I must go on. I can't go back. I do find much in Father Baker's *Holy Wisdom* that I find nowhere else. He seems to tell you the steps one by one.

14 *December,* 1915.

" The Father Superior passed to his rest quietly about 6.30 this morning." That is the notice by Father Cary. I heard a bell tolling just as I was going to vest for Mass, and I knew it was an extra bell, so I ran downstairs and asked " What bell was that? " feeling a dread lest it should be the death of Father Maxwell. But the man did not know.

However, a brother came into the Chapel after I had commenced Mass and let me know what had happened.

As I went to the Library afterwards to do the fire-place
I was called to Father Cary in the Superior's room, and he
said, " You have heard of our great sorrow ? "   He was so full
of grief.   I could say nothing but bow, with the broom and
dust-pan and brush in my hands.

So we go to our account.   It was a very beautiful death.
The last I saw of the dear Father was on Thursday at Compline.   He came out of the Sacristy, where he had heard his
last Confession.   He walked down the Chapel to his seat
with his hands together on his breast.   He looked ashy white.
I have felt all the time I have been here that there was a
mysterious and inexpressible change in that face.   This is all
I know.   He probably went to bed late, never to rise again.
Last Sunday morning he preached a remarkable sermon
upon " Even so come, Lord Jesus ".   His theme was that
we had lost the old lesson of Advent—the apostolic expectancy
of our Lord's immediate coming in Glory.   For himself, he
dreaded to think He might come at once.   He was not ready.
He narrated something from a Retreat of the Father
Founder's at Cuddesdon before his Ordination—How a
priest ought always to say Mass with that expectancy.
He ought to be prepared for the Host and everything to fall
away and JESUS Himself to appear.

I sat by his side at dinner last Sunday and he talked
quietly to me.   " Had I got accustomed to my lonely life?
What time did I say the Night Office?   Did I undress each
time?   You say it in your habit?   What time do you go to
bed? "   and so on.   The last time I spoke to him was on
Thursday after None.   I asked if I might go out to get my
hair cut.   He first said, " Yes, I suppose you may!   Have
you any money? "   Afterwards he arranged for me to have
it done in the house by one of the Brothers.

The end is terribly sudden for the Community—and a
great shock.   That is a very heroic and unselfish way of
living.   But one does regret some things about it, because one,
rightly or wrongly, wants that goodness prolonged in the
world.

One turns to the future.   What meaning has it for us, for
me?   He was a supporter of my hopes and I had taken his
counsel a great deal and he had encouraged me.   Now I am
left absolutely alone.   Before this there was a sort of appeal
to Father Maxwell.   That is withdrawn by GOD.

15 *December.*

I am quite content to die here or even to go back to S.D.C.

if it is GOD's Will. But to do the latter would be moving *backward* to me.

5 *January*, 1916.

I am reading less than at first, as I find the desire for prayer has grown and I give more time to it. That I am thankful to GOD for. On the whole, as I write, I am very free from the rather severe conflict I passed through.

I pray kneeling upright on the step of the Altar with nothing to touch. I trust GOD will give me strength to continue in that way. Did I tell you that I was driven back to read the *Fathers of the Desert* and that drove me to search for Cassian, so I am reading his *Conferences*.

My six months of weeks expires on April 15. So that the time of six months will end on Easter Monday, April 30. It may be GOD's Will I should stay on for twelve months, in which case I will gladly embrace that further time of loneliness. But it seems that the natural and simple thing would be to join whoever is waiting at Easter. . . .

I can't express what this time has been. At first it was such a joy to be able to get at books and read. That has passed and really everything has subordinated itself to prayer and the desire to pray grows.

23 *January*, 1916.

There is a real romance and force in getting up at midnight for Mattins and going to bed again. It makes the references in the Psalms a reality, too. I can see all that and love it, and it is worth all the strain. I am sure I can do it, and especially if there is a right arrangement in the Time-Table to fit it. I should always be regretting we did not do it, and in that way there would be scruple and the feeling we were not offering our best. . . .

To me it is of first importance that the new life should be hard. Forgive me. But do we not follow Stephen Harding? We shall have peace, and joy of solitude, and silence, and we must jealously guard against any lack of willingness to bear mortification.

And there is the additional help and inspiration in this direction which we must take to ourselves from the example of the soldiers in the war, and we must *use* it and get it into our lives at the beginning of our days. We must not lose the privilege of coming to the birth in such an age of heroism. We want all that splendid bravery and self-denial which the War has aroused and called out of a self-indulgent and pleasure-loving age. We want that *in* the Church, and we shall get it if we arouse it and call out loud enough for it.

For it is the same warfare, and demands ever the same heroism and sacrifice and hardship to beat back the evil spirits.

Very well. Let us have it in the new life tempered and safeguarded by the wisdom and discretion of our holy Father Benedict. I would rather have two or three men living like that for twenty years than a hundred with any sort of over-ture to softness. I don't suppose they will come in so fast. That will be best, so long as we get the right character at the start. Not an endurance that does not help prayer, but still an *endurance*.

Will you have thanksgivings offered for me for all this light which comes streaming in to guide me?

14 *May*, 1916.

Beyond the very war itself I believe the powers of evil are let loose and we *shall* feel the full force of all their rage and opposition more severely yet. There is certain to be a very real contest felt by those whom GOD calls to Himself in the way of mortification and prayer, and who attempt to make reparation by sacrifice.

The six months Father William was to be at Cowley were long overpast, but no steps had been taken as to his future, neither could he take any for himself. He writes on June 2, 1916:

Oxford.

I should like you to know that I am experiencing the greatest peace and happiness I have ever had. I think I have learned the lesson our Lord set before me, and I am in a very real sense perfectly resigned to whatever may happen to me and completely detached from everybody and every place. It is true I am the prisoner of the LORD, but I was never so free. GOD has given me the *Life*, and I desire nothing more. I am with our LORD all the time, having found His Presence in a new way. I am much more enclosed. There is a tiny little garden belonging to the Guest House shut off from the big garden. I am using that and have given up going into the other garden. The work I had in the big Library has been given to the new Novices, so I have no longer to go right through the House.

I am very happy, and I can go on like this to the end; in fact I wish I might.

Of course, I know it can't last, and that I shall have to go forth, but I am in no hurry for that. It looks as if I shall be here indefinitely—so be it. One thing I know, and that is that I must not open the door myself to go out.

All I need is the help of all your prayers, that I may keep

still and quiet like this in GOD. There is no sense of His disfavour for all my great unfaithfulness in the past. He has taken that completely away in my prayer and Communions.

There is the desire to be truly contrite and humble, and also to be kept in this same way of glad surrender and utter trust. And that is the substance of all my prayer now.

You will know what it has cost me—and will cost me yet—and you will know, too, that I shall have many a struggle to remain quite true and faithful to this in the long, long months that are to come. . . .

16 *December*, 1916.

I am not disturbed as to what you say about the solitary life should I go into a cottage and find myself alone. I could only bear it by GOD's grace and gift, but so far as I can judge myself, I think I should be supremely happy. I think the prayers of others would support me—that link which has sustained me hitherto and nothing else. As I think of the way I have come and what GOD has done, how He has left me here and given me the longing of the Cave, I am persuaded it is most likely that will happen. There is, in addition, the consideration of its fitness as being the truest way. And it seems that GOD has withdrawn the only (other) way—that of St. Bernard, who gathered his flock before going forth. I don't fear the food, etc.; I managed to survive in model-dwellings and I don't think it would be difficult. I only fear my own unworthiness and sinfulness.

.   .   .   .

I am sure the usual preparation and thanksgiving for Mass is right . . . but I like to have my own quiet prayer as well; that is why I want more time before Mass. I like also to go through all I desire to offer the sacrifice for, before going to the Altar. . . .

I am taking a great many notes from Scaramelli, and I can feel the good of it . . . Manning's *Eternal Priesthood* is one of the best books I know. . . .

But Father William could not remain indefinitely at Cowley, and the suggestion was made that he should look out for a cottage in the neighbourhood to which he might go for silence and seclusion, and yet be near enough to S.S.J.E. for help and supervision. The offer of a country house, or even of an Abbey with an endowment, did not deflect him from his resolve to wait until he could begin in quietness and seclusion. The Abbey, he remarked, would be " simply an extinguisher ". But the offer of a cottage, and then part of the vicarage at Radley, where he could begin with one or two companions, prompted more careful consideration.

24 *December*, 1916.   *Oxford*.

Father Bull has been talking to me about my affairs. I have now been here as guest for over twice six months, and S.S.J.E. give their approval to my going forward. The new Vicar of Radley has offered me the old part of his Vicarage. It is a double house, and the part he offers me is very old and has its own garden. He is acting as Chaplain to Radley College, and has all his meals in the College and spends most of his time there when not in the parish. He only uses two rooms in the Vicarage, and keeps no servants. It is quite secluded, and gives me all I need to live my life quietly till others come. In some respects it is the truer way of beginning. It is an act of faith in GOD, and it puts the life there for others to come into and it has Father X . . .'s sanction.

By the way, there is a capital wash-house and copper, but I think we ought to have a washing-machine. The work will be heavy for two old men! But it will be most delightful.

On December 22, 1916, we find he had written to a friend:

Mission House, Oxford.

Remember it may be a weary and troublesome journey for me yet. I know I am only human and very wicked, but the trials and disappointments only establish me and fill me with greater fire and zeal and, I hope, deepen my life. I could not turn back of myself, but I can let GOD push me back.

The failure of men coming immediately (to join me) does not really touch my life, except to prove my stability. Moreover, the paralytic waited thirty-eight years at the Pool of Bethesda before he was healed. And, of course, the whole foundation of the spiritual life would give way if you limit your endurance to five months!

January 4, 1917.

. . . I went to see the Vicarage at Radley. It would do admirably if I could arrange servers. It is very old indeed: probably a monk lived there from the Abbey at Abingdon, and I could have all the old part except the kitchen, which can be shut off. The Vicar is at present living in that himself. I could have it until a year after the war ends; then he will want it for a man he hopes may come as a gardener. So it fits in that way, too, as quite temporary, and I can have it free. . . . You will know I am really unconcerned and going on with my life quietly. If only I might be left alone somewhere and there be no more changes.

There had been full sympathy and understanding between Father William and Father Andrew in his office as Superior S.D.C. The election of a new Superior at the Autumn Chapter of S.D.C. led to some misunderstandings as to Father William's position, and so prolonged his stay at Cowley. He wrote as follows to the new Superior:

> The original arrangement was that I should come here for six months, and at the end of that time there should be an expression of opinion by S.S.J.E. as to the reality of my vocation.
> I have now been here as guest for over six months. S.S.J.E. give their approval to my going forward, but for the time being the way is blocked, as every man is claimed for war-work. Can I see you to discuss and obtain your approval of my next step?
> It is felt that no purpose is now served by my staying on here indefinitely, and I am naturally most anxious to discover another way of pressing forward. It is because any such step would be outside the last agreement made for me that I must needs ask your sanction for it.
>
> . . . . . .
>
> I need to live my life quietly till others come. In some respects it is the truer way of beginning. It is an act of faith in GOD, and it puts the life there for others to come into.

Early in January the new Superior of S.D.C. came to Oxford to see Father Bull, the Superior of S.S.J.E., about any further arrangements to be made for Father William. They discussed Radley, and in the afternoon Father William walked over with his Superior to see the old vicarage.

On the way he told Father William of the great strain that was falling upon S.D.C. The lay Brothers were being called up for the army; and with the Mission at St. Philip's, Plaistow, they were too short of priests to staff both Hanningfield and Stanford-le-Hope. Father William, with his instinctive generosity, offered to return to East Hanningfield to relieve the great need, and this with the consent of the Superior of Cowley. The Superior of S.D.C. accepted this, and wrote, " The Brothers were full of joy when I told them you offered to return to help us till the war is over ".

He bade Father William return to Hanningfield: to have a cell under the same roof as the Chapel, to do the needed Chaplain's work there and look after the Chapel. The spirit in which Father William returned for the last two years of his vigil was both comprehended and fortified in the following fine letter from the Superior of the Society of St. John the Evangelist, Father Bull, S.S.J.E. It is true that patience was to be well-nigh exhausted in this last period of waiting. But at length we shall see how, to use Father Bull's words, " the gate opens " so that " a safe advance is made ". By the mercy of Divine Providence it was not until the indications of God's Will were " made clear by Providence " that Father William went forth from among his brethren.

From Rev. Father H. P. Bull, S.S.J.E.

DEAR FATHER,
          This *present* time, while you wait, is indeed a time for strengthening your brethren. What you say about yourself is most clear and touching—and it may be that a little band will suddenly gather—and around you.

It may be also that your disappointment may be the kindling of others, as Father Benson was disappointed of his desire to go to India, that he might send a troop. He had to teach and inspire what he could not do himself—till he was old.

It was, however, his constant teaching that in the Providence of GOD we are to see the indications of His Will most clearly— " The circumstances of His Providence are the revelation of His Love to us and of the way in which He would have us love Him ".

The inward personal calls are tested by the fulfilment of the obligations of His Providence.

Your own acceptance of present postponements is indeed the testing and purifying of your personal desire; and if you meanwhile heartily cast yourself into the duties of the present, and the needs of the present in your own Society, cherishing the inward spirit of contemplation, you must gain, as well as those around you.

In the end, as I am sure you realize, your dedication into such a life, however occasioned, as an act of reparation,[1] must rise higher and purer, as a dedication which has no other than its own character as its motive.

---

[1] Father William, as is made clear in several unpublished letters, had offered his life in reparation for the collapse of Caldey, whose ideal had been in some respects similar to his own.

An act of reparation is that which, in the judgement of a generous heart, seems to us fitting, and because it is generous love it may well be accepted; but GOD's ways of reparation may well be other than ours, and in the sense of " sacrifice and meat-offering Thou wouldest not ", He has no need of them.

I have added this, because I should fear, lest in any act Godwards, what we were doing, or what others failed to do, became a dominant thought, instead of only an occasion of that which at last had to be undertaken in the pure region of the Spirit—the response to the Love that desires all. Our reparation indeed for our own failures in response, our recognition of the Glory that excelleth.

But this will all be the development of that of which the genesis was what you describe.

For the moment I feel that your identification of yourself with your Brethren—to supply anything that you can—is the guarantee to yourself, as to them, that the persistence of the desire of a more perfect renunciation is of GOD, because self is put away, and then as the gate opens, a safe advance is made.

But the issue is so great a one that we may not hasten it, save by our desires for it in itself and for itself. " For His Body's sake "—Yes, but for His Own Sake still higher. For with Him exalted in us, the health and healing of His Body on earth is secured.

Yours affectionately in our Lord,

H. P. BULL.

VIII

RETURN TO HANNINGFIELD

The Gate Opens

God restores gifts to those who are faithful in the time of His withdrawal.
(His) gifts become brighter to us in their joy when we have experienced their
temporary withdrawal.

R. M. Benson, S.S.J.E.

Enough has already been said of Father William's life at Hanningfield to enable us to envisage him again in his old surroundings.
It is clear from letters that he returned there in February 1917
and was again transferred to Stanford-le-Hope in October of
the same year.   On his way from Oxford to Essex, Father William
stayed with his brother in London.

He writes from there, February 3, 1917:

> I am thoroughly convinced that I am in the right way of
> God's Will.   It is very marvellous to me.   He has preserved
> me and brought me through most dangerous things.   I have
> miserably failed in the midst of the dangers and in upholding
> that which He placed in my care.   It seems that in His love,
> He has now removed every obstacle, and I have only to be
> faithful in my own life and He will bring it to pass.   I am
> so glad to be where and exactly as He has ordered, and there
> is no sort of disappointment or regret at returning here
> for the present.   I am thoroughly satisfied, and there is
> great assurance that He will do all for me, if I will only
> keep quiet and faithful.   I don't think I ever desired to
> scheme.   I know I get very enthusiastic, and that carries me
> into activity when I ought to be passive.   I only desire
> to live my life faithfully and strenuously and I can go on
> waiting indefinitely.   The more I wait, the stronger I get.
> No!   the money did not disturb me in the least, and I am
> only afraid I am not sufficiently grateful for it.   But these
> matters are quite apart from me personally, and have become
> more than ever the mere appliances God would use on behalf
> of men generally as they gather together in devotion to Him.
> It may well be that another will have the burden of handling
> them. . . .
> My supreme happiness is to be one of the family and I

shall be a better member of it if I may be in subordination for the moment. . . . I am *satisfied*, and I can be content to do nothing and say nothing—only to try to be a better man and learn to pray more faithfully. That I may do if I leave off peeping at others except to love and help them, as I am in that sense subdued, and at last comparatively still. GOD bless you for it all.

It was a joy for him to be once more at Hanningfield—to love and help the leper patients and the staff. His Superior refused permission to have with him a young priest who had been praying for six years for an opportunity to live the Contemplative Life, during which time he had said the Night Office in preparation for the fulfilment of his hopes, and who asked to join Father William at this time.

In spite of his strenuous work he found time to read during these months. There is a letter written on Whitsun Eve (May 26) 1917:

I have enjoyed *Mary Teresa* and *The Praise of Glory*. The latter especially is a wonderful example of what is set out by Poulain. It is a living treatise and a most beautiful life, but it makes one feel what a little way one has travelled. I have learned a great deal from it even now. Certainly it has led me to see one thing very plainly: I must *not* look round so much, but be content to be where I am and wait for GOD to lead me to Himself. There is a flood of light in what the Father said to Sister Elizabeth when she confided in him her desire of suffering. He told her not to limit herself to that, but to yield herself in all simplicity to GOD, leaving Him free to act in any way He chose. Of course I meant to do that, but I have failed dismally. More and more I come to feel there is really only *one* prayer. Now I must bring all into harmony with what I begin to learn by shutting out everything that is not His Will.

So, you see, I have had my conversion.[1] GOD has indeed blessed me and brought me into a life of Prayer and silence. I will try to be more faithful to that, and leave the rest in His hands utterly. I won't pry into the future again. That will wreck my life. There is all I need here, with just sufficient touch with others to save me from being self-centred. I can be happy in the truest sense and content.

If He lays the burden of founding a Community upon me, I will try to rise to that, but He will surely bring it to pass

[1] An explanation of the sense in which Father William uses the word conversion at this time will be found on p. 142.

in His own way, and I need not cast about to discover the next step. I shall rather find I have been placed there without knowing it. Whatever burdens come then will be sweet to bear and fruitful in the New Life. If anything happens I can take it to Father George and let him tell me what to do. I can always plead for my life if I am truly living it, and it is only out of that that anything *can* grow. I see that; seeing it afresh in its simplicity fills me with new peace and happiness. It is all I can offer to GOD.

This Whitsuntide I then again beg your prayers, that I may begin once more to be faithful to my conversion. GOD bless you more and more.

To the Same.

19 *June*, 1917.   *East Hanningfield.*

I think and pray a great deal. . . . The key of the position seems to be in *patient waiting*. I am waiting before I write to Mr. W . . .[1] Even if he pressed for us to begin and waived the Latin, I should fear asking the Superior to reconsider my position. I like the patient waiting best—that gives time to weave something under which it would be natural for the new life to develop without the break of going away. . . .

I always come back to patient waiting. It seems to be the right way, because it leaves me in the hands of GOD, and He can bring to pass so many things that are beyond our powers.

14 *July*.

When the time comes to speak, GOD will show me what to say . . . I can't feel it is time yet. . . . I can only wait where GOD has put me. . . . I must trust GOD to complete the deliverance He seems to have begun. . . .

I am busy cooking in Brother X's absence. It is a good experience. . . . Please let me have your notes soon. I could use them in preparation for the Retreat and Rest. I have been devouring *Holy Wisdom* again. There is none like that. Father Pearse is saturated with it.

Towards the end of October, Father William was sent to Stanford-le-Hope to share in the work in the kitchen and on the land and to take charge of the adjoining parish of Fobbing. It was here that at the end of November he heard of the death of Harold Lloyd, who was killed in the advance of the Egyptian Expeditionary Force on Jerusalem.[2]

[1] Mr. W. proposed to join Father William.
[2] Harold Lloyd was killed on November 6, 1917, and was buried later in the Military Cemetery at Gaza. The stone Crucifix in the Garth at Glasshampton was erected in his memory.

Mention has already been made of this young layman. He had lived for two years at the old Parsonage at Pleshey in the hope of being one of Father William's first novices. When he first became known to Father William he was uncertain of his future and had litle knowledge of the Catholic Faith. They met on the railway platform at Worcester, both waiting for the same train. Father William invited him to stay with him for a week-end, and Harold, not quite knowing what was expected of him, wrote asking what he should bring. Father William replied on a post-card, " I should bring a collar-stud. William S.D.C." A friend writes, " I remember Harold showing me the card at Pleshey, where he was then living alone in the Old Parsonage, and telling me it was his first realization of what detachment meant ".

He had a true and deep vocation to the Contemplative Life and Prayer, and had he not been killed in Palestine he would no doubt have gone to Glasshampton. On hearing of his death Father William wrote:

27 *November.*

I have been expecting to hear Harold had laid down his life; nevertheless it is a great grief to me and pierces me with sorrow. I am radiantly glad for him, dear boy.

I won't write more. . . . I feel a great desire to be still and to be alone here. It is so beautiful that you have a Requiem, and I hope to say one quietly on Thursday. I am a weak mortal, and for the moment one side of me is crushed. It seems very wonderful, for is it not another assurance of GOD's purpose? Surely an Order such as the Monastic and Contemplative Life could not grow out of anything more intensely real. It plants itself where it *can't* fail and come to naught, and it creates here at the same time something in harmony with its dedication to St. Mary at the Cross. . . .

1 *December,* 1917.

After the great grief of receiving the news of Harold's death I do not seem to have lost him at all. He is there in my thoughts and prayers just as he ever was. It was entirely a supernatural friendship from the beginning, and it can't end because he has passed within the veil. That happiness that came to me lately began at the time of his passing, and there is certainly quite a new still joy I never had before. He fulfilled a long time in a short time, and I am thankful GOD used me to accomplish so much for him.

I was not relying on him to begin, though I looked forward to the time when he could join me. I am not relying upon anyone to begin with now. I think I have always felt that yearning to go forth into the wilderness *alone* and live as a hermit. That is still my truest instinct. But I do not hug that. I look at all that comes. . . . If I were free at this moment and left alone I should go into the desert—I know that. It seems to me that if God gives me grace to live the old life here faithfully, He will lead me into it.

He wrote to a friend about his daily round.

14 *December*, 1917.   *Stanford-le-Hope.*

I am not depressed! I feel any trials because I am sensitive, but in a sense it is right that I should feel and suffer. But I have no unwillingness to bear it, though I often fail. . . . All the time I am quite content to abide here and die if it is God's Will for me. I don't get much time to myself now, some weeks I am all the morning in the kitchen cooking! I spend the afternoons doing the work in the garden I have set. I can't manage to break the night, so I rise at 4. I get to rest about 9.30. There is also plenty of house-work, so you see it is by no means light, and I get tired and feel the cold very much. I read from 7.30 till Compline at 9. You will know that one's frailty makes the disappoint-ment of there being no possibility of beginning harder, but I try to make an offering of what the conflict with self costs me, and I can truly say God gave me grace to bear Harold's loss with resignation and joy, though I could not help great grief.

In the spring of 1918 it seemed to Father William that the time had come when he could claim the long-sought permission to retire to the life of monastic enclosure. He was now fifty-six. It was four years since he had first made known to his Superior his interior sense of God's call. The lack of priests for the work of the Community was now over. In the previous November two priests and two lay Brothers had been professed and set free for work at Plaistow. There were thus now five priests at work where normally there had been only two or three. He could not but feel that the need to relieve which he had offered himself in January 1917 was now relieved. And—what seemed a further providential indication of God's Will—just at this moment the last of the many offers of houses came to him; a furnished house with a gardener was placed at his disposal. In March he wrote to the Superior asking permission to begin his life of enclosure.

Now came the darkest hour of all. The Superior of these years had consistently and on principle opposed Father William's aspirations from the beginning. He was one of those souls who envisage profession in a community as involving a bond to the family of which it becomes a member, the indissolubility of which is the same as that of marriage: one is vowed to *it*, rather than to the will of God as found enshrined within it. Hence he did not feel himself able without further deliberation to continue the policy of his predecessor. The principles established in consultation with Cowley [1] were set aside; and Father William found himself once again present at a prolonged discussion in chapter as to the reality of his vocation and the possibility of his release. He made an appeal to the brethren, apparently without avail, to abide by earlier decisions. The years of patient waiting seemed to have been wasted. His own struggle (like that of his nation in these months) seemed to be closing in defeat.[2] He could only state his own conviction that " having fulfilled the test set me, the Community has no canonical right to prevent me going forth to live a stricter life ". It seemed to him that the right thing would be to go forth, though it would be a bitter grief to go without the affectionate dismissal of his brethren. Nothing was to be gained now by smashing down a door that had for a year been open. He did, however, desire the understanding of the Warden and the blessing of his Bishop, and to secure this wrote to the Bishop of Chelmsford on June 17, 1918:

> I write to ask if your Lordship will be kind enough to grant me an interview for the purpose of submitting to you the grounds upon which I have decided—after many years trial and consideration—that it is right for me to leave my present Community in order that I may go forth in obedience to the Call of GOD to live a stricter life as a Religious, in prayer and silence and work of a different order than is possible in S.D.C.
>
> I am more convinced that GOD calls me to this different work and mode of life than I was when your Lordship kindly welcomed me some years ago. I have not approached your Lordship since then, for I have had no definite opportunity given me to begin that life, but at last the time has come, and I desire to lay before you the difficulties I have had to meet

[1] A memorandum embodying these is amongst the papers relevant to the monastery at Glasshampton now in the care of Father William's executors.

[2] Father William's first letter to the Superior of S.D.C. is dated November 1914, just after the beginning of the four years' war. His first night at Glasshampton was November 18, 1918, the week of its close.

and overcome and those which still confront me.   I am clear
that at 56, if I am to begin that life, I must do so now:
that it is a Life which many men are seeking as they come back
from the horrors of war, and that there is a very real work
to be done among them, other than that of social and
democratic reconstruction.

I am not at the moment desiring to approach your Lordship
as Visitor of my Community; but as a priest who has been
most of the last sixteen years in the Diocese, and is now seeking
your counsel and help before taking a step which, after prolonged consideration and prayer, I am sure I must now take
if I am to be true to GOD's Call to me.

He wrote to the Warden, Father Frere, C.R., in a similar strain,
and he asked his friends in Religious Communities to pray for
him, and also that obstacles might be removed from the way of
four of the men who had been hoping to join him, one of these a
priest.   In the course of his letter to Father Bull, the Superior of
S.S.J.E., he said:

The Bishop of Chelmsford (Bishop Watts-Ditchfield), in
asking me to justify a life of prayer, sought to know if I had
any plans!   My answer was that I had no plans; I only
desired to be faithful to what GOD asked of me, but I could see
at the same time that very much indeed must spring out of
that faithfulness to the call to prayer and discipline which
would mollify our sores.   He was anxious to know what I
meant, and I mentioned what I told you about men leaving
S.D.C. for the monastic life at Downside, and I remember
I also said I believed such a life, when strong and established,
might bring forth a penitentiary for fallen priests.   While I
can see all this, and know it is inevitable because it is within
the Church even now, it is not that which I seek.   I seek to
go forth alone to a hidden life of prayer and mortification
because it is to that only that I know GOD calls me, and I
must leave the future with Him.

To a Religious.

22 *June*, 1918.

. . . I go through a great deal of mental agony, but my
Mass this morning brought me great joy and consolation.
. . . I saw that it may be GOD's Will for me to be only a
voice in the wilderness—to be used, unworthy as I am, to
prepare the way—that I must decrease and suffer for the
Truth's sake and perhaps be a martyr for this cause.   I gave
myself for that or anything GOD wills.   It is in keeping with
my original offering of myself as reparation.   I have made

many mistakes and am guilty of much wilfulness and sin, and please GOD I may have the grace to bear the penalty. . . . It is very difficult to know at times when it is right to act. It seems to me one must do some things, even when one would prefer to be still. You know more than anyone that I did not seek this vocation. It came to me, and when it was held out I recognized it was a sort of sequel to much that I had experienced, and then I firmly put myself to the test and submitted myself to the judgement not only of my Superiors here, but also of S.S.J.E. . . . I can't see where I have been wrong, except in being anxious to make a start. . . . If I were a stronger man and a saint I might walk out now, but I fear the reproach of . . . and it would overwhelm me, and I could not expect men to come to an outcast. It may be my way out is *in* this darkest time. . . .

Out of this darkest time the dawn did come. Before the August Chapter he had addressed a last appeal to his Superior: Providence had spoken once more in the offer, not of a house, but of a stable.

To the Reverend Superior S.D.C.

May I be allowed to ask the Chapter by means of this for permission to go into a very simple stable cottage at Astley? The owner, Rev. Cecil Jones, who is in great sympathy with my desires, has placed it at my disposal, and the Rector, Rev. David Proctor, would give me a very hearty welcome and I should be quite close to him for Confession and help.

The stables belonged to a house long since burned down, and a part of these have been converted into a cottage of four or five rooms, and the rest can be developed when and if necessary.

I should be most grateful if I may have the consent of the Chapter to begin now in this simple way and in utter poverty. Mr. Proctor says the cottage is " ideally secluded," and that it is about a quarter of an hour's walk across a park to the Church, and he invites me to go to view the place in August, when Mr. Jones will meet me there.

The reply of the Chapter was a resolution passed by the Fathers and Brothers that Father William be sent forth " generously and lovingly ", and though he had still three months to wait for this to be confirmed in the Autumn Chapter, he was free to make such arrangements as he thought best. There is a joyful letter to a friend in which he says:

You don't know the tremendous joy it is to me to contemplate the life alone in utter poverty. It thrills me. I don't say it will be easy for me, but I know it will help me more than anything else. It is an unspeakable privilege of which I count myself unworthy. I am convinced of its being the right way, if I can escape to it.

At the Autumn Chapter, on October 3, 1918, a new Superior, the Rev. Father Barnabas, was elected. He had always been in sympathy with Father William's ideals, and as the following chapters will show, his sympathy and help did not fail him in the years to come.

To those whom he had asked to pray for his vocation during these many years of patient waiting Father William wrote:

My release was granted by the Chapter, with the Warden in the chair, and a sympathetic Superior who voted for it, on his right—

WE PRAISE AND THANK THEE, O GOD.

PART III

MONK

IX
GLASSHAMPTON: THE STABLE

" Give me the lever ", said Archimedes, " and I will move the world ".
The prayer of the desert, disinterested, adoring, humble, contemplative, is the
lever whereby Christ the Head, and His members in union with Him, moves
the world.

The Guardian (Leader, March 12, 1943).

ONE word as to the name of this third section of our book. There
can be little doubt that Father William lived as a friar and
later as a solitary. But that his life was ever properly that of a
monk some might question.[1] St. Benedict would have been more
indulgent (see Chapter I of his *Rule*), but he wrote before there
was any distinction between monk and solitary. However, even
if we restrict, as has become the tradition, the use of the term
" monk " to the *fortissimum genus* (the securest kind) of monks for
whom St. Benedict wrote—that is, to coenobitic monks (monks
who have a life in common)—Father William certainly finds his
place amongst them, " The Coenobites—that is, those who in
monasteries live under a Rule or abbot ".[2] Certainly Father
William for twelve years, 1918–1930, lived a communal life in a
monastery under a rule; and that rule was his very strict interpretation of the Benedictine Rule in its Cistercian development.
He remained at Glasshampton until in 1936 (the year before he

---

[1] A normal conception is as follows:

> A monk may conveniently be defined as a member of a community
> of men leading a more or less contemplative life apart from the world,
> under the vows of poverty, chastity and obedience according to a rule
> characteristic of the particular order to which he belongs. The word
> monk is not itself a term commonly used in the official language of the
> church.
>
> *Catholic Encyclopaedia*, X. 487b.

[2] Rule of Saint Benedict, Chapter I. He goes on to speak of the solitaries
as " the second kind " of monks.

died) ill health made departure imperative; but the last years before he left were spent largely in solitude. After eighteen years of life spent as a friar at the disposition of his community, he spent eighteen years in the place where he was installed by his Superior. Surely a monument of stability.

Father William was set at liberty by the generous decision of his community to make such arrangements as he could for his future life. And he had to make them alone. The men who had looked to him were scattered. The war was still going on. The body of Harold Lloyd, who would have been his most trusted companion, lay in the cemetery at Gaza.

But Father William was never less alone than when alone with God, and he went on quietly with his preparations. His letters show that he had been guided to what was truly a " place prepared " for him and one which he was now free to make his home.

> I have thought of the Bishop of Worcester. Should I decide to ask him to receive me, I think I could get someone to write to him for me. Mr. Jones [1] might help me to find a cottage on the Malvern Hills, and I might go to the Bishop to receive my confessions. Mr. Jones is rich, and he is convinced of the need, so he very likely would offer me a cottage if it was suggested to him. If he helped me it would be a reason for asking to see the Bishop. I should plead just for an Altar and his blessing for my own life of reparation and for English Mass and Offices and poverty.

Later he writes:

Stanford-le-Hope.

> I am in touch with Sir Sydney Lea at Stourport and David Proctor, Rector of Astley, both near Hartlebury, where the Bishop of Worcester lives. They are looking for a cottage. There are no cottages near here or Hanningfield to be had for love or money. Do pray much for me.

And again:

> I have indeed fallen among friends! Mr. Cecil Jones owns land at Astley, and has seen Father Proctor. There is a stable which belongs to a house long since burned down, and it has been converted into a cottage. I can have that I think and it can be adapted and added to when necessary. That is perfectly lovely. It is secluded.

[1] Chaplain of the Convent of the Holy Name, Malvern, and the owner of Astley and Glasshampton.

Father Proctor is a great saint. We had talks together years ago when he desired the Religious Life, but he found he must undertake the education of his sister's children.

To be near him and in a stable is ideal. If I go into the stable alone to begin, I shall be under the direction of one of the best priests in the Church of England.

The Rev. David Proctor himself wrote:

DEAR FATHER WILLIAM,

I have known for a long time of the desire that is in your heart, with which I am very sympathetic and have prayed much about it. I have spoken to Cecil Jones, the chief land-owner, and have suggested to him various plans. He is coming over to consult me on Thursday, so will you please pray that we may be guided aright?

Yours affectly in Christ,

DAVID PROCTOR.

Later. Cecil Jones and I have been to look today at the disused stables about which he has written to you. I think they are practicable for your purpose, and capable of development. But you had best come over and see them.

It was thus in August 1918 that Father William first saw Glasshampton, the place which was to be his home for nearly twenty years. Buried in the depths of the county of Worcester, the Welsh and Malvern hills in the distance, stands the Park of Glasshampton with its glorious trees, in the heart of which once stood an isolated and ruined stable, its ruined, high-walled garden, and at a little distance away the fishponds of the monks [1] who once dwelt here.

The stable is no longer. Converted into a monastery under Father William's hands, it remains the silent witness of his faithfulness and devotion to God's call and his faith that what had once been the home of men dedicated to God's service would be so again.

Doomsday Book tells us that " this Manor called Glaze was

---

[1] The monastery known as Astley Priory was an " alien monastery " founded in 1087 by the monastery of St. Taurin of Evreux in Normandy. The monks were Benedictine. A long document dated A.D. 1316 of considerable interest to historians deals with a dispute between Astley Priory and the vicar of Astley, " William, perpetual curate of Astley ". The monks had been reducing the tithes due to the vicar and his appeal against this was granted in the Bishop's Court. The sentence may be examined in Canon Wilson's edition of the *Worcester Liber Albus*, S.P.C.K., 1920.

formerly held by Ulmar who could go where he would ". It has changed hands many, many times. For a long period it was the property of a Benedictine monastery, but in Henry VIII's reign [1] it came into the possession of the Blount family. They were followed by the Winfords, one of whom was knighted by Charles I in recognition of his zeal in the Royalist cause: the last of the Winfords, a spinster, left the whole Astley estate to a distant connection, the Rev. D. J. Cookes, at that time curate of Astley. This fortunate, or unfortunate, cleric seems to have had ample means and determined to make his magnificent inheritance still more magnificent. Not satisfied with the splendour of the house, of which local tradition declares it had as many windows as days in the year, as many doors as weeks, as many chimneys as months, he decided to renovate or rebuild the entire structure. This he did, and he seems to have added stables—those stables in which we are now so interested. But in the spring of 1810, when the house was practically finished, a careless workman let fall ashes from his pipe, and Glasshampton was burned to the ground. [2] " It was a judgment on me ", Mr. Cookes used to exclaim, " the Lord knew I could not have kept such a place going ". Upon the offending workman, Lee, no judgement fell. He became one of the most brilliant oriental scholars of his time.

There remained only the lovely walled gardens, parts of which are still to be seen, and the chain of fishponds with their shading trees, and the stables with the entrance through which to drive coach-and-four into the great courtyard.

The house was rebuilt, but again to be burnt down the very night before a great company was to assemble for the house-warming.

In the nave of Astley church lies a flat stone " To the memory of John Dawson, [3] architect of Glasshampton 1707 ". This is all

[1] Is it a significant coincidence that the first version of the catechism issued in this period of the spoliation of the monasteries omitted the words " thy neighbours' house " from the commandment " Thou shalt not covet "? (For a brief statement of the facts see *The Church Catechism Explained*, by Arthur M. Robinson, D.D., p. 76.)

[2] Wedley, *Twixt Severn and Teme.* Shuttleworth Press, Kidderminster.

[3] " In John Dawson we see another Shenston, not as a poet, but as a lover of the beautiful with a power to adapt natural advantages to lofty ideas. To this man we owe the beautiful chain of lakes. . . . Not only the lakes and the lovely walks, but the great house itself was the emanation of his fertile brain. The only picture of this beautiful house is to be found in the pictures of Nash." Op. cit. p. 20.

there is on the stone. A like simplicity characterises his extant work.

At the time at which Father William first saw it, the stables themselves could hardly be said to be there; only one corner of the quadrangle was habitable. Here the gamekeeper had lived for some years, leaving it because it was considered unfit for human habitation. At the time of which we are speaking bats and owls alone inhabited it. It was this ruin which Father William was to transform into the present monastery. It is true he found on the spot bricks such as are not made today and timber not yet rotted away—the material with which he first began to build.

But however ruinous the stables, Father William at once saw in them the answer to his prayer. He left Stanford-le-Hope in October. He writes:

> I am to leave here on Friday. I am thinking of November 21 (Feast of the Presentation of our Lady) as suitable for the Blessing of the men's first House, and the Superior has promised to try to come. They have just dispatched a load of furniture from here for Glasshampton. It is a painful and trying time—the more because they are so kind and generous.

After he left, the newly elected Superior, Father Barnabas, wrote to him:

> *October* 12, 1918.
> I purposely remained in Chapel while you went away, as I knew you wanted to go as inconspicuously and quietly as possible. But I knew that in the sympathy of silence we were giving each other our goodwill and blessing.
> Between now and then will you let me know for certain whether the House is to be blessed on November 21, so that I may mention the hope of my being present to Chapter?
> I trust you will happily settle down and see more and more clearly the unfolding of the Will of God.
> > Yours ever affectly,
> > BARNABAS, S.D.C.

Father William's first impressions of Glasshampton must be given in his own words after he had seen it, with the permission of his Superior, at the end of August:

> The stable is not a bit like I pictured it. Much larger, and forming a quadrangle with an entrance through a large gateway with turret and clock above. It is very severe but good: built over a hundred years ago. It is in the

midst of a huge park, with only owls and jackdaws to disturb. It is most beautiful country, like Wales, and the stable stands high in the hills, the Malverns in the distance.

Mr. Jones, Father Proctor and I went together to see it, but before doing so we said the *Veni Creator* in the beautiful Norman Church of Astley.

All the estate belonged to a Benedictine Priory, and there is the Prior's Well [1] and the five pools for fishing close by. I am to have it for nothing. It is just to be white-washed. Father Proctor wrote to the Bishop, and I am writing now.

To another friend Father William had written a fuller account:

The part I am going to occupy is one side of a quad. It backs upon a warren or wood, which extends a mile or two. There are trees close up all around; the ground falls slightly at the front, and everywhere else is parkland. I could not take it all in properly, but it is large and spacious . . . rooms very lofty. . . . One could put a cloister right round inside the quad with lawn and Calvary in centre, and all could open into the cloister. There are no doors on the outside of the building. When the gate is shut, all is shut in. I want a big bell for that gate, and a big letter-box. There is a small door in the gate. There are sort of square towers at the corners, one of which it struck me would be part of the Chapel, and the other the library. I am sure it can make an ideal monastery. There is water. . . .

My heart is very full, but I can't write it!

The following letters were written by Father William to a Religious who could enter into his thoughts and desires; one professed many more years than he, to whom he could appeal for help about many things; what Office Book he should use and so on.

There are other letters in this section to those who undertook the provision and supervision of material equipment to which he could not attend owing to his solitude and the inaccessibility of towns and shops.

The letters give a vivid and attractive picture of Father William, alone in the great park, at first in an empty and derelict stable. The rats, the " potatoes popping in the oven ", his getting the monastery into working order with only " one pair of hands " to unpack everything, scrub the floors, do the washing and fetch

[1] This well in the ruins of the garden still supplies some of the water to the monastery.

the milk; groping his way to church every morning across the park and down into the valley, where he had to cross the running stream, sometimes losing himself when the snow had obliterated his landmarks. But the letters tell the story best themselves:

St. Edmund, November 20, 1918.

> *Glasshampton Stables,*
> *Shrawley, Worcester.*

I slept here last night for the first time, but did not actually sleep much. I think the rats scented an inhabitant, and some of the potatoes I left in the oven kept popping and jumping about. There were strange noises, anyhow.

But it is so sweet and blissful, and such a high privilege! I have been very busy washing all the furniture well and polishing it up a bit. I heard today the Archdeacon will bless the House tomorrow week. (So it *is* within the Feast of Our Lady.) He bikes over from Hartlebury Rectory for 8.30, and he will say Mass. I expect Father Proctor, Cecil Jones, Father Barnabas and Sir Sydney Lea, and I shall have to give them all a pittance afterwards. I am hurrying up the Altar and the luggage from Stratford.

I have got the carpenter on the estate to put me a letter-box and fix a bell. There is a big bell in the turret over Entrance-gates, and he is putting a rope to it, so I shall ring out the Angelus presently. He must make me a little dresser for the kitchen and a few other necessary things. The place grows on me very much.

E. W. is likely to get his release soon, from what he says, and I must see about a cell for him to come into. There is no room for another as it stands. He will lodge out at first. That will be my rule, and he may not, of course, come till after Christmas. . . . Nevertheless, I must soon begin to move to make room for him and others. I shall speak to Cecil Jones next week when he is here. I have thought it all out.

I am having the present Chapel dedicated to St. Bernard. That will always be the Blessed Sacrament Chapel. There is a fine lofty place that will make a splendid Chapel for Choir and which can have (conveniently) a Narthex for externs. I must include that in developing for the next cell, for you pass through the end of it to the most suitable part of the building for cells. It is at one end of the Square. Each end has a sort of square tower; this one is not like the others inside. It has no upper floor. It only needs the roof, ceiling and the brick walls rubbed down and a cement floor. Upon that I should erect a stone Altar. And there is some capital woodwork in the Stables well-seasoned that will make a dado and seats. I will draw a plan for you. I have reserved the Dedication to our Lady for that Chapel.

Feast of St. Cecilia, 22 November, 1918.

It is cold here because the rooms are so nice and lofty—12′ 6″! You can imagine the height of my proposed Chapel, which I should think well over 20 feet.

I am getting up at 4, instead of at 2, because my tortoise stove is not here yet and the place is icy cold at 2. I get up at 4, and go and light the kitchen fire first—there is no fireplace except that and a small one in the Library—then I shave and have my bath. I say my Offices in the kitchen before a big Crucifix, and leave for Church at 6.30. It is downhill into a great ravine filled with rocks, and the brook rushing over stones, across the bridge and then up and up to the Church. It is like Devonshire—almost like Morwenstow. I get back for pittance at 8.30 or 9. The fire is in and the water hot. . . . The water comes from the brook, and is sandy, so I fill a great bath the Rector lent me and let it settle, and then bale it out clear for use. . . .

The list of things to come include all I shall ever need. You *shower* good things upon me. No table-cloths, thank you, I have one Miss Butler gave me for guest house, which I shall spread for the breakfast next Thursday.

I am having the Choir-boys and the boy from the next farm for tea that day, and shall get them to sing a Hymn in the Chapel and say the Lord's Prayer. The Rector thinks it good to do that.

I fetch my milk each morning from the farm. It is a nice walk and lovely scenery. They are nice people, and the man a Scottish Presbyterian. She is a Churchwoman, brought up in Stourport, and the children go to the Church School. I shall get butter there, too, but have none yet. I shan't be able to do anything to the garden for a week or two. Then I will spend some hours each day. There is a great deal to do yet, and it takes time to clean up and fetch in coal and wood and attend to water. I am to have a boy for errands and he will get the milk. . . .

24 *November,* 1918.

The two chests of drawers have arrived, and there is the consignment from Stratford waiting to be hauled up. Thank you for all the very useful things. I am so glad to have a lamp at last. . . . I have a letter from Father X . . . (S.S.J.E.). He can't come . . . but it is good that they should have suggested being represented, and shows I have their confidence.

It is such a help and strength to have one's absolution every Saturday evening. We make our Confessions after Evensong. Surely I ought to be full of gratitude for all GOD has showered upon me. It is a tremendous responsibility, and I need all the prayers I can get to be faithful. . . .

I can see that in all probability GOD has led me to Father Proctor as my future Director. In every way he is apparently the best priest I know. I have been able to see a good deal as I lived with him, and he is a *wise* man. I have asked him, and he has agreed to be my executor for the time being. I have told him why—that everything, including the two policies, is for the Men's Contemplative Community. . . .

The Rector has given me a cat.

(These letters are all signed William S.D.C.)

Feast of the Dedication (*November* 26, 1918).

It has been a great day. I can't realize it all. It was so still and quiet. I had a strenuous time getting ready for it. All the things seemed to arrive together. The Altar and the loads from Stratford and the fixing of the Stove all came tumbling on the top of one another, and only one pair of hands to unpack and set in order. Then, too, they came to get out the potatoes in my enclosure, and I had to give them all refreshments.

I had to be up early to get breakfast. I gave them Quaker Oats and Bacon, Tea and Coffee, etc., etc.

The Archdeacon is a man of much prayer and quite Catholic. He took the Order and prayers I suggested in Alb and violet stole, and then changed to white and put on Chasuble for Mass, and I served in *rochet*. They all four came together soon after 8. Father Barnabas was very sympathetic, and said it was a joy to be present, and Cecil Jones seemed delighted, and I know the Rector was full of inward joy. I must show you the Altar if I can (drawing). There are white holland curtains right round hanging from iron rods fixed to the four large posts, which have candles. Then there is the back of the Altar, into which the Tabernacle is buried, and the Tabernacle has door and rod and key gilt. The Altar fits in beautifully, and looks simple and dignified and most devotional. I have a lamp hanging at the side to light when the Blessed Sacrament is reserved, and a carriage clock which strikes, on a bracket, and a hanging lamp on another bracket with socket. This is high up, and lights the whole very well. There is a very good rug (from St. Stephens, Bristol) before the Altar, and three stools I had made for Catechism at Bristol. Yes, there is also a credence. That is all.

The Larder and linen-room come next to the Chapel, and then the Library and Refectory, which also serves as a Sacristy; then Kitchen and my cell. I have a Mop to clean lobby and Refectory. It does very well.

The view from the three windows is across the Park, which falls from the house and then rises again, and you see the Church perched on the highest ground beyond. The great oak trees are magnificent—close up to the house—and the cows are there grazing. . . .

I am going to have lockers to form seats inside entrance. The mud is terrific. The iron mat just the thing.

Then six boys came to tea, and Francis Mason, a delightful boy who helped to whitewash the place, came on his way home at dusk. I took them all into Chapel, and we sang "*Jesus meek and gentle*" and said *Our Father* and *Visit, we beseech Thee, our homes*, etc., and the Blessing, and I gave them a card each. It was all quite simple but beautiful.

It has been a very happy day. The Rector says he will come once a week so that I can say Mass. And I hope soon to have our dear LORD in the House with me.

Well, the cat is black, with a white star on his breast. I think of calling him or her Star or Stella. I shall be so glad to have one for Harold's sake. . . .

Later.

I want a good saw to saw down trees and a hatchet; a spade and fork for gardening, a trowel, a hook-shaped blade for hedging—also wheel-barrow, rake and hoe.

A hard mattress? Straw palliasse if possible.[1] I ought to have two. In fact furniture for two.

Advent Sunday.

I have just rung out the 12 o'clock Angelus. I found there is a bell in the turret, and I have fixed a rope and commenced to ring Angelus after the Blessing of the House. It is a good bell, and sounds miles round.

I said " sit down *at last* ", because this last week has been one continual movement. I thought I had escaped from it all on Friday, and when I had cleaned up after the previous day—though weary!—I sallied forth soon after 3 with that monster saw and proceeded to make faggots of a fallen tree just outside the stables in the park. I had nearly filled the

---

[1] The Carthusian beds at La Grande Chartreuse, as a visitor saw them in 1924, when the Abbey had been secularised by the French Government and was open to visitors, consisted of an oblong box of good width and depth into which a loose and thick straw bed was put. Such a bed is free from draughts and not over uncomfortable. Father William's own bed at Glasshampton was very hard and narrow, more like a prison bed.

wheelbarrow when I spied a man approaching. He turned out to be a young sailor, and he nearly dropped of fatigue, for he had walked the long way round from Stourport, and besides his kit-bag he had a loaf of bread, etc., and an overcoat and waterproof.

Well, he is a youth I prepared for Confirmation, etc., at Bristol, and he had discovered my whereabouts, and had written saying he desired to give his life to GOD as a thanksgiving for his safe deliverance in the war. . . . I wrote and told him he could not come to see me, as he asked, as it was a most inaccessible place and I had no bed. . . . But he would not be put off, and wired saying he was coming by the first train on Friday from Bristol, and come he did. . . . I took him inside and gave him a meal, and then took him to a cottage about two miles off (my Guest House at present). He was at Church at Mass next morning, and made his Communion, and then came up here. . . . We had a long talk, and I gave him dinner and sent him back to his mother. He seems very determined, and I did not discourage him. . . . He is only 19, but he carries the *Imitation* and *Spiritual Combat* and a Rosary with him. He says the Rosary when on duty at night. He has been in the barrage off Dover. So you see that pleasant incident went to fill to the brim a very full and eventful week. Please pray for him.

Father William's training in an architect's office stood him in good stead; he saw at once where he must have a door knocked through, where he must have a buttery-hatch, how he must have gutters put up to keep the fabric dry, and so on. And he was very practical in small matters. He swept the chimneys—full of birds' nests after many years dereliction—by the simple device of cutting down a young poplar, lopping off the side branches, but leaving some twigs at the top.

It was just after the war; no wood to be had. But he found beautiful wood used for the mangers in the stable. He had no proper tools. He writes: " I had nothing big enough to turn the nut, so I hit it round with a hammer and the little crowbar ". But at last he got his wood. From this he made seats for the big Chapel and found he had sufficient to floor the Narthex for visitors.

The following letters are to the two friends who were acting as trustees for the money given to begin the foundation:

I must have a door knocked out from the kitchen to the wash-house. The mud is awful, and there is much traffic to the wash-house. I keep coals and wood there and clean and fill lamps and clean boots, and it is where I unpack everything. . . . It is easily done, as I will show you on the plan, and is of *permanent* necessity. Also there must be a buttery (or whatever you call it), *i.e.* a hole to pass the food etc. from kitchen to Refectory. That too is easy and permanent. . . .

The floors of kitchen and my cell are not fit to stain and very difficult to scrub and keep clean, and can never look respectable. Therefore I think I must get linoleum down before another man joins me, if the place is to be like a religious house should be.

I have got the tortoise stove fixed in Chapel, but now there must be a hole knocked in east wall near ceiling for ventilation. . . . You can't pray in bad air!

I spoke to Mr. Jones about the need of some cells, and he quite approved of my scheme. I think I must do the cells and the passage through to them *at once* and leave the Chapel for the present. The present Chapel will serve quite well for three or four men, and we can get on with the big Chapel at leisure and by degrees.

There are no rain-water gutters, so the rain drops from the roofs on to the ground, which of course makes mud all round the outside of house, and besides it causes the walls to become damp. . . . It is necessary for health's sake to put up gutters round the inhabited parts at least, and some tubs to catch the rain, which is of such service, as the water is full of sand. . . . I can't very well ask Mr. Jones to do all this. He lets me have the place for nothing, and I can see his men on the estate are very pressed on account of shortness of staff. Can you let me draw on the fund for these things? I ought to put them in hand at once. I don't want these things going on when the men come. It must be so far ready for them, and unless it is healthy and convenient the order of the house will be impaired. But what I have enumerated will suffice for many years, and you may rest assured the place and surroundings are well worth the outlay. . . .

Stella has arranged to have a family. She is very merry, and sings all day long. . . .

I had a load of coke arrive on Saturday. The horse was a monster, but he was steaming all over and dripping with perspiration and going like a bellows. So you may imagine the difficulty of getting things hauled up, especially now the ground is soft. . . .

It is pitch dark as I go to Mass, and some days you can't see an inch in front of you. That is when the lanterns are so necessary and useful. . . . I got a long way out the other morning, and found myself in "Toad's Hole." . . . It was as bad last night, you could so easily go over a precipice into the brook or on to the Rocks.

. . . .

There are some window-frames I can use; two are quite ecclesiastical. . . . They will do for the Chapel. And I am saving what doors I can find. But it nearly makes me weep to see the vandalism and how the place has been allowed to go to rack and ruin. All the roof must be overhauled. The other side of the quad is bad just because the roof is broken through and the wet pouring in. I must save that later if all goes well.

I just dipped down into the wood the other day and looked up at the building. It really stands on the highest ground, and you look up at it from the wood and see a severe building which could not be anything else than a monastery.

I am going to put a fence round our garden to make an enclosure. It will be of the trees I have felled. Little piles driven in and the thinner branches intertwined. . . . And I must do that round the building, too, to keep the cows at a little distance. They make much dirt.

I can manage about vestments. S.D.C. gave me some, and some came from X . . . I have a very large Spanish Chalice, but it wants regilding inside before being used. . . .

. . . .

What an interesting parcel it was that came on Saturday morning. The country postmen rather kick at parcels, and no wonder, you would say, if you saw the roads up to this place. He cycles as far as he can. But I started by giving him hot coffee and bread and margarine on a little table, with a chair to sit and rest. So we are good friends. He is a great tall man, and very pleasant. The man who brought my coke was in a fearful rage. But I said I liked a man who *felt* for his horse, and hot coffee and a table and chair made us friends.

It is so wet, and the Deer Park is terrible! Did I tell you I got a Sou'wester oilskin coat at Stourport, like the fishermen wear? I saw it hanging at the door of a shop, and at once I was covetous! It goes down to my heels and catches all the rain and mud, and I wash the mud off periodically.

I have written and asked my brother to come down and look at the place, and if he will come we can get out a scheme for the whole block before touching anything, and he will watch the estimates for me. . . . In the meantime, men are waiting as you see by enclosures. . . .

Advent III, 1918.

Sunday is my day for writing letters, and I have only just sat down to begin at one o'clock. I have been fully occupied ever since 4 a.m., except breakfast at 10 a.m., and I am truly weary, but that is blessed, and can be offered up together with His weariness. I would not have it otherwise; I should soon feel the life was an unreality. So I have lit a fire in the Refectory. I have hardly had any fires at all, it has been so warm, and I do not sit down except for Offices and meals. I can't get time for reading yet; that will come presently, and I so look forward to it. At present I *must* practise the " Glory of going on "! I think perhaps the aching in my left arm may be rheumatism, though, as you know, I am left-handed, and that arm has had some heavy labour. I have had to sweep the chimneys. I did it with one of the trees I have felled—a poplar, I think. I left some twigs on the top, and it went right up the chimney, because of course they are not very high. I did it in the orthodox way, with covering in front of grate, and down rattled the soot as I twisted the tree about.

Then I have been taking to pieces some of the woodwork of the mangers, as I can't get any wood for love or money, and there are all sorts of things to be made. Well, I almost grieve to take the work to pieces. I never came across such splendid work; it must have cost thousands of pounds. I have been working at one of the sides of the mangers. . . . I got the post away after unscrewing a big nut. . . . I had nothing big enough to turn the nut, so I had to hit it round with a hammer and the little crowbar. . . . Then I could not get the boards off the iron bar—it gripped them like a barnacle, so I had to saw each board near the bar, and at last got my wood, which is $1\frac{1}{2}$ inches thick. It was a herculean task!!! but I did it.

Another feat I accomplished yesterday was this: I started to clear the mud away to make a path from gateway to my entrance. I had the wheel-barrow to fetch bricks and rubble and a lot of old tins and broken crockery. To my utter surprise and delight, I soon found that the whole courtyard was once cobbled. At any rate, I have taken away about four inches of earth—very muddy—right from the entrance to house, to the arch of Gateway, and it is all cobbled!!! and I found the sink which originally drained courtyard. I shall proceed to remove the rest of the mud by degrees. Remember this is wholly the work of *worms* (for 100 years), of which I found millions. . . . I don't know how far the cobbles run, for potatoes have been growing over most of the

courtyard. . . . I shan't have vegetables *in* the courtyard.
I want a big Calvary in the centre someday. Neither shall
I have a lawn; it would take up too much time to keep
in order. I shall have either shrubs or fruit trees, I
think. . . .

Advent IV, 1918.   *To a Religious.*

I do want to send you a loving message from this Stable
for the Nativity, and I can't find words to clothe it, but
it is a very intense greeting from a very full heart, and
you will know how my thoughts will go out from my
hermitage to you as you gather in Chapel and recreation.

I had to put up a line in the wash-house because it rained
so incessantly. I foolishly trusted to one nail already there,
and when the line was full of beautifully washed garments,
out came the nail and down came the lot on to the floor!
I left them and went into Chapel for my Office. When I
came out I enjoyed rinsing them out again.

I have done some butter-beans and green peas. The secret
of cooking seems to be that you keep on boiling and baking
something all day long, and the more you cook them the
better they are. But my oven refuses to bake. . . . I have
hardly any coals. They only gave 10/- worth! I am
writing for more. I dare not start the Chapel stove. The
only chance of getting them up now through the mire is the
neighbouring farmer's team of horses. . . .

I had finished my letter and broke out again. Now I
must close what is to be my Christmas letter to you. I can
only hope you will charitably read between the lines and
accept the warmth of my greetings, which refuses still to
show itself. GOD bless you. GOD bless you. Amen.

Yours affect. in our dearest Incarnate LORD JESUS.

WILLIAM S.D.C.

To friends and Trustees, 31 *December*, 1918.

How I have wanted to write to you! And first for the
magnificent packages of useful things which were hauled up
here on Xmas Eve after my vicissitudes. A boy came first
to say the cart, which also had some second-hand furniture
I had bought upon it, was stuck in the mud and could not
get any further. But fortunately the builder was here—
a great big man (too big for the weighing machine of the
Local Enlistment Board)—and he had his horse and trap and
kindly sent a man with his horse to the rescue. They just
managed to deliver at dusk before the builder and his men
left. I could not resist looking through the things before
I laid aside everything and went to Chapel.

Oh! the brick dust and the muddle! I resolved to touch nothing on Christmas Day, and came back after the Sung Mass and lit a fire in the Refectory and tried to forget the dirt and confusion everywhere and read and mused. . . .

The doorway to wash-house is done and the hole from kitchen to Refectory, and they make a huge difference. Then I have had the sailor lad for two nights and days!

I have my brother coming tomorrow, and as soon as he gets out a scheme I will get an estimate for the three cells. . . .

I have been reading St. Benedict's Rule and the Commentary on it. I much like the idea of putting St. Benedict's Rule in front of our Rule. It is a sure foundation for any Rule we may make of our own.

3 January, 1919.

My brother is taking measurements. . . . I am very busy cooking for him and the boy who holds his tape. He thinks the place perfectly ideal for the purpose. . . . I shall be so glad to have the sailor to relieve me of the journey to Church and much of the work. But I have been glad to have the experience of being alone.

Eve of Epiphany, 1919.

I am enjoying a fire in the Refectory after having enjoyed the beautiful Offices. I was to say Mass at 6.30, but I lost myself in the dark and snow. There was nothing to guide my feet, the snow had covered my landmarks. So I wandered round the Park a long time, and though I heard my Mass Bell, I could not respond. And down I went into the snow. . . . I said as I was outstretched and my Office Book and lantern went flying, " O dear LORD, do help me! "

I got to Church and found the Rector reading the Epistle. I was wet and my hands numbed with cold. But I took off my oilskin and pulled down my habit and went and served the Rector. I was able to get a wash at the Rectory, and was as warm as toast and had a beautiful time before saying Mass at 8. I got back, I suppose, about 9.30. Luckily I had some hot water and Quaker Oats on the little oil stove, and after giving the cat her breakfast I had some tea and the oats.

Sir Sydney Lea and his children and my brother were at my Mass, and my brother is dining at the Rectory. He has worked hard at the dimensions, and I got the builder up yesterday to meet him. I am afraid it will be a considerable outlay. We must put the roofs right first and get the gutters up. I am asking for estimates for all to be done up to and including the Gateway and Turret. I wish we could do it all now and get in the hot-water pipes to spare us the dirt and distraction later when men are here . . . and I think altogether it would be more economical to do the whole thing right off. Prices won't go down, they say, for four or five years at least.

It would give us five rooms, the Chapel and Sacristy and the room over the gateway. I have had an inspiration. To turn my personal cell next kitchen into larder and use present larder as Sacristy. It would do admirably with a chest of big drawers for vestments. . . . But it will take all the money pretty well to do it, though we can secure that it provides a really good permanent Chapel. And my brother will see the work is done well. The brickwork is splendid and in perfect condition. As you approach it, it gives the impression it was only put up the other day. . . . The other half is in not so good condition. The roof is very bad, and so the timbers are going. . . .

There is no doubt it is the right place, and I feel very strongly it should be made as right as it can be for living the life freely without the hindrance of the want of proper rooms. It would be an ideal Monastery in ideal sur-roundings.

Feast of Epiphany, 1919.

The Rector came up to see me this afternoon, and I went round with him and explained it all, and he said " Yes, you must make every effort to push the work forward. I can see its importance."

I should be sorry if it was all self-chosen, but it has so grown out of a wonderful over-ruling of GOD's guidance in every way and after such long waiting and many prayers and Novenas that I am confident it is GOD's own way. It is so unlike what I anticipated and so infinitely better. . . . It seems to me right that I should let you know my own confidence and the Vision of the future GOD gives me. In these wonderful days it should not be surprising that GOD should use us to build up the walls of Jerusalem and restore His Temple. I do not say it should be exceedingly magnifical, but it should be worthy of that which it is to enshrine. . . .

To a Religious, 15 *January*, 1919.

I propose putting the men into Retreat for a period when they arrive, i.e. after a day's residence to shew them about.

Mr. Cecil Jones came. He will send me a letter stating that the place is given for the monastic life. Not given to me or us. It will not be our own, but we shall not be turned out. . . . He is going to fence us in all round to keep out cows and mark our bounds. . . . I think he is glad about it. . . .

The Retreat for men as they arrive seems to send them into silence and to GOD at once, and I can keep them there when it ends.

16 *January*, 1919.

One can hardly be a guide to regions one does not traverse oneself. The real strain and contest comes because it is so extraordinarily difficult to keep wholly supernatural as one fingers the material. It is what produced the Hermit and the Cave surely. If I read aright the priest (especially) has missed the highest when he marries. The highest for many is marriage but the priestly vocation is to the highest possible.

24 *January*, 1919.

St. Timothy (my birthday). I had a Mass in the house, the Deacon serving . . . I am 57 alas! . . .

28 *January*, 1919.

E. X. comes the Sunday before Septuagesima and the sailor comes when I bid him. I shall have to prepare a careful Time-Table for them both.

A heavy fall of snow! The country round about outside looks superb. The workmen are very slow, but they are doing the work well, and I can't tell you the difference it will make. . . .

To Friends and Trustees.   12 *May*, 1919.

It is very kind of you to order the tables. I want *big* ones, please! at least 5 × 3 for kitchen and another quite as big for laundry. If we have one big table to sit round in Refectory it ought to be say 6 feet long by 3 feet, but it is more correct to have long narrow tables going round wall of Refectory. The size of Refectory is 16 feet by 11 feet 6 inches. Yes, straight legs. . . .

I can get sufficient greens now for myself and I have got all the seeds in. I mean of vegetables etc.

The builders are very slow, but I must be thankful to have even that. . . .

16 *May*, 1919.

The cells are getting on. They are simply charming. I am reducing the cost of heating to the very minimum without jeopardising its purpose.

27 *May*, 1919.

There are no flowers in this park now nor round me. I

generally take a trowel and basket when I go out, and bring in roots of ferns of cowslips or ragged robin or primroses or bluebells.   The vegetables are coming on splendidly.

2 *June*, 1919.

Yes, we must go as GOD guides.   I am not happy in being alone, except that I have not chosen it.   I can see that men would not be content to be satisfied with what would satisfy me, and indeed unless they were very wonderful they could not live and grow in the house as it was, but I must not lose faith and confidence, and I am sure companions will come.

23 *June*, 1919.

I am in the new Chapel, and it is such a delight.   So big and lofty and spacious.   I had to have the part below the beams whitewashed.   I am very anxious about the expenses. Can you tell me exactly how we stand and how much I can spend?   I want to have the bell-turret made water-tight to save clock and beams.   It pours in when raining.

17 *August*, 1919.

We had a deluge as I was at Confession yesterday.   My new Rain Water butts were " christened ".   It did not last long, but it was like a new experience after drought, and reminded me of Elijah.

My few flowers are a great joy—the mignonette grows here most luxuriantly and wafts its odour into the house.   I have thrown heaps of poppy and foxglove seeds about for next year.   Any seeds you can send out of your grounds would be doubly acceptable.   You know I have two or three apple trees, one is a Blenheim, I am told.

The Chapel is so simple and spacious and airy and lofty and quiet, in fact it is perfect.

6 *September*, 1919.

H. L. is settling in and is I think quite hopeful, though he does not commit himself to anything beyond being a penitent seeking to know GOD's Will for his future life. . . . He says already he would be sorry to leave here!

I must go on with the English, I think, and hope a complete translation of the Benedictine Breviary will be forthcoming. Everything has come in such a wonderful way that I have great assurance that this too will come in GOD's good time. I think I can see it is what I must stand for, though I can see the other way as well; all those who think of coming seem to desire English and they are priests. . . .

I would not object to people saying their prayers in
Latin if they were saturated in it from childhood, but I
can't bring myself to believe it does not matter if they
don't understand what they are saying—that is the real
point. What is done privately is altogether a different
matter and it would be wrong to deny the use of Latin in
private to those who know it and rightly love it. . . .

There is a growing appreciation of the House and
surroundings.

It *is* monastic and yet quite simple. H. L. says it is
extraordinary monastic and he is charmed with the whole
setting. . . . There is a great deal to thank GOD for and I
don't think I can see it all yet.

26 *September*, 1919.

. . . Thank you for two beautiful Crucifixes which arrived
this morning. There is a case at the station too, but I
have great difficulty just now in getting anything brought
up. The tables etc. are still at the farm at Astley. . . . I
suppose it is the harvest.

I have heard from Mrs. Lloyd that the body of Harold has
been exhumed and buried with great reverence at Gaza.
There is a cross and full particulars put over it.

X

THE MONASTERY OF ST. MARY AT THE CROSS, GLASSHAMPTON

An instant of pure love is more precious to GOD and the soul and more profitable to the Church than all other good works together, though it may seem as if nothing were done.

SAINT JOHN OF THE CROSS.

ABOUT this time, the end of 1919, Father William drew up the following proposed dedication of Glasshampton as a Religious House and the Time-Table which follows.

CONTEMPLATIVES OF BLESSED MARY AT THE CROSS.

A Congregation of men, priests and lay, dedicated to GOD in the life of the Counsels for a life of SILENCE, CONTEMPLATION, INTERCESSORY PRAYER and MANUAL LABOUR.

The Congregation shall consist of One Order, priests and laymen, according to GOD's freely given grace of Vocation. Laymen who are its members shall abide in that state of life wherein the Vocation of GOD found them.

SILENCE. The Rule of Silence to which all the Brothers shall be bound shall be perpetual and unbroken excepting at Mass and the Divine Office and Corporate Recreation, of which there will be three in each week. There is always freedom of speech between the Superior and the Brethren for spiritual purposes, Direction and instruction.

MANUAL WORK. It is the purpose of the life to embrace, besides the full Divine Office and two hours mental prayer and intercession, five hours manual work or its equivalent each day.

ENCLOSURE. The Brotherhood would not usually leave their enclosure, but one day a week all shall go for a walk of 2 hours. The Silence shall be maintained and they shall walk together, i.e. within sight of each other.

95

TIME-TABLE.

2 a.m.	Mattins and Lauds.
6.	Rise.
6.20.	Prime and Chapter of Faults.
7.15.	Mass.
	Terce.
8.15.	Pittance.
	Meditation and Mental Prayer 1 hour.
9.30.	Work.
11.30.	Sext.
12.	Dinner. None. Washing-up.
1.30.	Recreation 1 hour.
	Work.
4.50.	Cup of Tea.
	One Hour's Prayer.
7.30.	Supper. Washing-up and Work.
8.30.	Compline.
9.	Retire. Greater Silence.
9.30.	Lights Out.

Father William kept this Time-Table himself till his death, saying the full Offices for the day and the Nocturns for night, though unable in the last years to *rise* for this, owing to ill health. Men came and went, but, as always, the majority were the sinful and the failures. Attracted by his personality and compassion, they came not to a *monastery* or a *Life* as such, but to the Priest-Religious who had made the monastery. Having found healing and help, they moved on, but there were very few who did not write constantly and look back with longing eyes to the life they had shared, even though they had only partly understood it. There were priests also, some who had tried their vocation in other Religious Houses who came to look for help and sympathy, but not the fulfilment of vocation. Perhaps the life was too austere for them; more probably they had not the single eye, the one end and aim which was Father William's.

Austerity was to him not an end, but a means to an end. There is a revealing sentence in a letter of December 1921, " It is cold and we have put out the furnace and *feel a touch of the cold of the manger* ". And when he had no money and an empty cupboard he was not the least dismayed—" My cupboard is bare, but I will not stock it till God Himself provides the wherewithal. We go on hand to mouth and I am quite happy at that."

From the beginning he foresaw the possibility that he might

die alone, that no sons might come. He knew his venture must at all events be of slow growth; that it was a venture not calculated to attract. It had nothing to show to those outside. As he so often reiterated, its very hiddenness and inactivity must add to its long period of probation. It was wholly a work for God. "I yearn for sons," he writes, "but I am always trying to suppose I may die childless, and it makes me set to work to get my own life right, that there may be that first obligation well satisfied when I render my account." And if men did not come, "That is not *my* responsibility but *His*. I believe this with my whole soul!" He rarely mentions de Caussade in his letters, but there was surely never a greater example of absolute abandonment to the purposes of GOD.

> "It is always difficult", he writes, "to go on with nothing to show. People are so liable to think it is another experiment which has failed. They can't see that there may be something hidden which GOD is blessing all the time. We within, who see that, find it difficult to keep up our hope and trust, so it is no wonder that those outside are so slow to have confidence."

During Lent and Passiontide of this coming year he was finding with our Lord the way of the Cross. The men who came to him were not the men he would have sought. He writes: "I have not yet found a true monk!" Neither was there the companionship in the true sense of the word, of men of the same spiritual attainment and growth as himself. He had been training himself for the life for the last sixteen years; for the last four years, and in particular during the period at Cowley, he had accustomed himself to the discipline of the life of a monk. Not even priests who aspired after the life could *begin* where he now naturally found himself. The tragedy, if tragedy there was, lay in the fact that a group of men similarly called and like-minded with himself had not begun together and lived together, sharing their first efforts and failures, and growing together into the life of the community. Community life cannot begin with a Solitary. Father William, himself naturally drawn to the life of contemplation, had grown through the years of vigil and waiting into the capacity of its highest form; the life of solitude.[1] He was in his daily life too far advanced, and too much alone. The men who

---

[1] Saint Benedict, Holy Rule, Ch. 1. Saint Thomas Aquinas, *Sum. Theol.*, II. ii. 9. 188, art. 8, speaks of this life as, from one aspect, the highest.

now came to share his life found it the life of a man of nearly sixty years, a life matured by experience and crystallised in form. Whatever the cause, he had his Via Dolorosa, and he trod it faithfully with his Lord.

Feast of St. Bartholomew, 1919.

I have had another delightful gift. The family of the Chaplain of St. Andrew's Home, Fulham, who died last week, are giving me his library complete. It is probably very good indeed, as he was a great student and a Catholic. There are about 1000 books. I shan't know where to put them and it is the beginning of the need of a proper library and study room. I am sure you will help me to thank GOD for this wonderful present. I am so glad because it seems that priests are coming rather than laymen, and it will be an assurance to them of some possibility of reading. It is a good beginning of a future big Library. . . .

I have begun on my vegetables. I mean to eat them. It is all the difference in the world to last winter. Now I can have a magnificent vegetable soup : carrots, turnips, onions, parsnips, tomatoes, parsley. I have three chickens and a cockerel and I am getting a young sow this week. There is a capital pig-sty, and it will interest my man, and moreover will I hope help to pay his wages as time goes on. I have a lot of things growing for the pig. . . .

Writing of possibly renovating the further " pavilion ", Father William says:

The chief point that sways me is that there *are* men who definitely say they will come. There are three priests and possibly a brother, and *if* they come say at the end of a year, there will be six. This is " counting " and they may evaporate ! but all the same they have all been to see me and write to me. I have only room for three of us, unless I sleep in the larder. I can go on till I am obliged to do that, and perhaps that is the right way. I am very happy as I am with H. L. I do not wish to do a thing unnecessarily, but there is time now for us to consider how to house the men if they come, and to be in readiness to proceed, since there is a genuine intimation of what may happen.

There must always be the element of a venture of faith because men who say they desire to come may change.

Mr. Hatherly of Smethwick has accepted the living, I feel a great relief. He was at St. Albans, Birmingham.[1]

[1] The Rev. David Proctor had resigned the living of Astley and entered the Novitiate at Cowley.

I have been here just twelve months. What a great difference it is to what it was when I came, and I am really glad to have companions for Christmas, for I am very human!

Bishop Gore's speech is magnificent!

December, 1919.

I am very happy. The long waiting for vocations and the trials with those who come and go is good for me, and it is the way GOD seems to point as the means of creating more material for a sure foundation.

I am prepared to be alone five years hence. It is only by being here alone and being faithful that a place and life can be formed for men to come into. I see how much GOD has done in the first year. Here *is* a Monastery ready, and I have gradually formulated a routine and exercise myself in keeping a Rule, and I can feel myself being trained and, please GOD, growing.

Looking back, I see I said I must not be tempted to be concerned as to whether men came or not. I must live the life myself alone and the rest must be left to GOD. The Chapter granted me all I asked for, and it includes that. It is this frank and open basis that makes me happy now. I simply go on asking GOD to send all things necessary and especially to raise up true monks, and I am often asking Him to let my life and prayer avail, though so deficient.

There is another thing I am so happy about. It is the sympathy and understanding of the Superior of S.D.C.

Wherever I look I see GOD's gracious hand, and I feel sure all He asks of us is faith and patience, and toil and willingness to go on through everything that may happen.

GOD bless you.

Lent I, 1920 (*February* 22).

This is Monday. I could not get on with your letter yesterday. You see, I have to be everywhere and do everything and just put C . . . on here and there and take him off again if he does not do it right—and then I do it myself again for a time. I find he does better that way, and it is so bad for me to keep on finding fault and it depresses the men. So I have come to the conclusion that I must be the slave of CHRIST in that way. It is a great thing for me to have learnt that and to have the strength to carry it out. It was a very great disappointment at first and I shrank from the toil of it, but now I see it is the only way. I must go in front and set the example and keep up the standard and create the right spirit in the house. Men have got so dirty and slovenly and untidy in the Army I suppose. I find it is making the impression I want and there is more care and I think the lesson goes home, but it gives me hardly any time for writing and reading.

I have got up the Figure of the Crucifix behind the Altar in memory of Harold. It makes the Chapel very devotional.

They are making great progress with the Infirmary end and I hope to get them on to the roofs next. The roofs will cost £300; they are very bad and must be stripped.

20 *March*, 1920.

I have had great refreshment in my Masses and prayers lately . . . much heaviness and depression is lifted and I am enabled to lift myself up to our dear LORD and there is an increasing drawing to His Blessed Mother. And I want you to know that light has come to me too in this way. All the life—the work—the Office—the Mass and even the men seem to be falling into a new one-ness. The old disconnection and apparent separateness has gone and there is a wonderful peace and calm I have never felt before. *All* has fallen into place and the whole is one and linked up together with better recollectedness. . . . I hardly like to write of this in case I lose it all. . . . I have, too, a strong presentiment that there will be a gathering together of a little family this year. [Here follow particulars of several men who might come.] It is like a little stirring of the waters of the pool. And it is somehow linked up with my own soul in prayer . . . everything seems like nature, ready to burst out into leaf and blossom. I am sure there is GOD behind it.

Did you ever read the Life of Blessed Louis-Marie Grignon de Montfort? It is a wonderful two volumes. . . . He was the bond-servant of Jesus and Mary.

In the spring of 1920, the Right Rev. Ernest Pearce was appointed to the Diocese of Worcester. On his coming into residence Father William saw him, and later sent him the Office books used at Glasshampton. He received in reply the following kind letter, which established the stables of Glasshampton as the Monastery of St. Mary at the Cross.

19 *June*, 1920.

I am much obliged to you for sending me the books, which I will look through as soon as possible.

I shall always be glad of the talk we had together here and shall take an interest in your venture of faith at Astley.

The facts which you comprise in your letter show that my predecessor wished you to do as you are doing, and the question whether the Archdeacon had authority to bless your

Chapel during a vacancy in the See is one which we need scarcely discuss, as it is understood between us that the Chapel is used only for resident members of the Community.

Please remember me sometimes in your prayers,

Yours most truly,

✠ ERNEST WORCESTER.

In sending a copy of this letter, Father William writes:

June 1920, *St. Peter.*

I hope it is a joyful Festa with you all. I am anxious to hear you got the copy of the Bishop's letter. I replied, " I beg leave to thank your Lordship for your kind letter . . . and for returning the Office Books, I had the pleasure of sending you to read. May I be allowed to express my warm appreciation of what you have said to me and for your leaving me, as you say, to go on quietly as I began with the approval of your predecessor ".

That seals episcopal *approval*, I think, if put together with the late Bishop's letters.

I went to see the Rector and told him that it gave me freedom to develop the life with the Bishop's knowledge and interest. He no doubt knows we have Reservation, as that is part of the life.   The Tabernacle was blessed by the Archdeacon, so I want to reserve *tomorrow*. The Rector agreed and now we have the Blessed Sacrament in our midst.

The men promise to complete the building and get out by the end of July and they are doing wonders. I fear there will be a big payment to make soon. I am so grateful to you for making this possible.

To the same.

You see all I see about the Bishop here. It is the hand of GOD upon me. *Now* I feel it is a real House of GOD. A Monastery with the Blessed Presence enshrined, and there is the lettering in gold high up, right over the centre of the Monastery and facing East.

" THERE STOOD BY THE CROSS OF JESUS HIS MOTHER."

That will appeal to the hearts of all who pass by.

(Letters after this are all dated from *St. Mary at the Cross, Glasshampton.*)

6 *November*, 1921.

This is Harold's year's mind you will have remembered. We shall have Wednesday's Requiem especially for him.

And it is just three years since I came into the Stables.

So there is Harold within the Veil and we are four trying to live the Life with faithful observance. If we can go on for twelve months together I think a little root will have struck.

It is quite enough to go on with, and the material seems of the right sort to mould and make traditions. As I look round at the Monastery and its present inmates I feel it surpasses all I ever hoped for, because the Life is somehow beyond what I expected and the home *is* Monastic, not Bohemian. So we can thank GOD and take courage.

I wrote a careful letter to Father X . . . I said the Life would be based upon the 3-fold ideal of Silence, Prayer and Labour, and Labour meant *hard* work in Garden and House, for no serious reading could be undertaken until there were more of us. . . .

We have done a lot of gardening in this lovely weather and made a great many improvements outside. It has been very good for us and we shall appreciate it all next Spring.

October 3, 1921. *St. Thomas of Hereford.*

I am busy today with washing and gathering apples. Such a fine harvest of beautiful apples, Blenheims.

We are going on very happily—more happy than I have ever felt and with the coming of S . . . there will be, I am sure, a real beginning of a little monastic family, and I am looking forward to our Advent and Christmas. . . .

I read and re-read Dom Butler and Delatte and am gaining a glimpse of the *Spirit* of St. Benedict. I read his Rule in rotation every day, and I pray to imbibe that beautiful simplicity and naturalness more and more. If we could only reproduce the Spirit which breathes through it all! I don't mean slavishly copy, but if we could touch his inspiration we should be very much like the ideal home of his vision.

I am rather encouraged because somehow I have always had that idea of a family life made up of very simple souls, and I have so often wondered how it is we don't get hold of farm-labourers. I did get one such, Brother X . . . and he is professed now in S.D.C.

Writing of " the monk's foundation " becoming, as he hoped, an accomplished fact, Father William said :

It seems to be nearer realization now than ever I have known it. I hardly expected to go through so much and to wait so long. Quite unexpectedly it suddenly is here just as I had almost lost hope and it is as I first pictured it, with simple men—men you can mould. Yet it is a very critical moment, and I might miss it all if I am not alive to its meaning and if I don't rise up and seize what GOD holds out. So do give me some of the prayer of your valuable time on the couch in the sun. I want more loving patience and more sacrifice of self to take infinite pains in training each one separately in the whole Life.

Christmas Eve, 1921.

I am so busy. A little address every afternoon on Bethlehem and a good deal of domestic preparations . . . Father X . . . came to dinner on Monday for a few days' retreat which meant fire in Guest Chamber, so you can guess what Martha had to do! He went Friday morning. I am so glad he comes; it is what I desire and we are getting intimate. He says he gets what he seeks here and certainly he revels in it. I think he has missed his way and should have been a monk. He loves us.

No! Father Y . . . won't come. He misses his books round him and finds the journey too much. . . . So he says. . . .

It is beautiful Christmas weather here after the rain. It is cold and we have put out the furnace and feel a touch of the cold of the manger. The Divine Office is such a joy on these days. We shall try and keep our watch. . . .

St. Matthias (*February* 24), 1922.

(About gifts for the work.)

It has been wonderful how GOD has answered my prayers. I had almost written to friends to help me, and then I said, " No! offer the sacrifice of righteousness and put your trust in the LORD ", and I have found the needful come, but no more. . . .

My cupboard is bare, but I will not stock it till GOD Himself provides the wherewithal. We go on hand to mouth, and I am quite happy at that. I have paid my rates and have the money for the coal at the Bank.

Baron von Hügel said there were five or seven new Carmelite Foundations since the war. I was saying to Mr. Smallwood [1] *we* in the Church of England had not experienced any turning to the Religious Life. I believe it *is* coming and many other good things, but we may have to pass through a great deal first.

I yearn for sons, but I am always trying to suppose I may die childless, and it makes me set to work to get my own life right, that there may be that first obligation well satisfied when I render my account. I once thought that after the

[1] See footnote 2 on p. 144.

war there would be many who would leave the world for GOD, but I was mistaken, I think.

2 June, 1922.

. . . I expect I am weary myself—I know I am—It is the incessant grind in kitchen etc. I think and feel I want a day off. But I offer all that to our LORD and go on, but it does not take it away—it only turns it into the right channel and leaves me still weary. . . .

Commemoration of St. Paul (June 30), 1922.

It is a blessed privilege to wait upon GOD and to stand aside in the dark doing nothing except trying to be a little less unfaithful. I must not rush in and *do* something myself because these three years have not established an Order. When one is wicked and restless it is hard to stand alone, but when one is surrendered and still, one can be gratulated, for it is perfect bliss!! I can hope for a blessing somehow if I go on hiddenly where He has brought me. Anything *I* do will eventually perish.

I will write more later on. This in the kitchen as I cook!

So the life at Glasshampton went on its even way. There were comings and goings of men, and Father William needed all his natural buoyancy of character and what the world would call " optimism ", but this fundamental characteristic, had it been alone, would not have carried him through. His hopefulness was rooted in the conviction that God had not brought him through all the past to leave him to perish in the wilderness. Yet as the years went on he came to realize that though the vision was true, the colours in which he had pictured it were not altogether of God's Will. That he followed the vision to the end, though the colour of the outline changed is the proof that what he had seen was of God; and as he rose up to accept God's Will through the hopes and disappointments of these years his own character deepened, and he found in his acceptance of God's Will as he came to know it by experience the strength he needed to fulfil his own vocation.

In the summer of 1922 a suggestion—not for the first nor for the last time—was made to him that he should join the Benedictine Fathers at Pershore. The following letter explains his position and why he regarded such a step as impossible. His soul was at home in the Cistercian development of the Benedictine life, and he felt the attraction of the Carthusian life, but he would have found it very difficult to be a monk in charge of a parish or to live the Benedictine life with a college for boys in the precincts of the monastery and as part of his normal work. The idea of prayer and manual work, enclosure and retirement were too deeply associated together in his mind in his ideal of the monk and the monk's life. It was because he sought this life, and had not found it in his day either with S.D.C., or in the revival of the monastic life at Pershore and Nashdom, that faithful to his own vision, he remained at Glasshampton and died a solitary.

Octave Day SS. Peter and Paul (6 July), 1922.

I think there are two distinct ways of living the Benedictine Life. They are both legitimate. I should like to stand for something Pershore does not stand for; but in standing for that I am aware it is the *least* acceptable in our day and that it will therefore be of slower growth. It has nothing to show to those outside, and its very " hiddenness and inactivity " must add to the long period of its probation as it spends itself wholly in the " Work of God ". I believe there is very little difference now in the Church of England in this respect to the time when Dr. Pusey and others began the revival of the Religious Life for women. They could not get it to " swing " without utilitarianism. But I am persuaded God wants what I would fain stand for and that it is the greatest need of the Church. Being where I am and having come to it as I did, I must stand by it even if I die alone. God may in His mercy raise up *the* man for it and bring him here for me to serve. I don't know. I can only go on trying to do my best.

The rest is not my responsibility, but *HIS*. That is exactly what I believe with my whole soul.

I sent the Indian back to Ireland on Monday. I kept him as long as I dared. I think he would have gone completely mad if he had been a day or two longer. You can't imagine his antics!! poor soul. I love him.

27 *July,* 1922.

Don't ever think I am going to do anything violent! If God gives me grace and strength I am going on just as I am and where I am till I die. After all I have two novices and we are really living the life in its fullness. . . . I try to discover how I can make progress, and that of course must begin in my life and prayer. If it were not for my sinful self, I should feel the difficult path I have trodden, and now walk in, is the very best and most hopeful. I know you pray that I may persevere in it and that all I do may be used by GOD.

.   .   .   .

I yearn for big troughs! We have suffered greatly the last two summers for lack of water, so I am putting up some huge Rain Water tanks in wash-house to conserve all the wonderful water GOD sends and I let run away. It will supply kitchen too.

GOD *will* send men sooner or later. It may happen, and probably will, just at breaking point. I indulge sometimes by imagining they are coming across the park. What matter if it only comes to pass after twenty years. It is not our business, but GOD's Will.

30 *October*, 1922.

F . . . & S . . . are here, so we are six, and B. E. . . . comes this week. You will think of me much in the next few months, for I have a great deal to go through and I am beginning to feel my age. The Doctor came and examined me. I have gastric something and have to take Bengers, *not* at 3.30 as he prescribed. . . . It is after morning pittance I suffer. No other time. It may be the long morning in Chapel, but I shall never give that up. I would rather die. It is *the* Kernel of the Life. But don't worry. I am going to rest more. I am teaching S . . . to cook. It is good for him. He needs that I should be much at his side at first.

.   .   .   .

We stand for something no other Community stands for, not even X . . . Quietness, hiddenness and simplicity, Prayer and labour and Silence—nothing else. It *is* a difficult time . . . there have been so many disappointments. But, thank GOD, we are getting a few years of tradition behind us, and after a few more years of slow and steady progress we shall have won the confidence of a few. It is always difficult to go on with nothing to show, and people are so liable to think it is another experiment which has failed. They can't see that there may be something hidden which GOD is blessing all the time. We within, who see that, find it difficult to keep up our hope and trust, so it is no wonder that those outside are slow to have confidence.

I am so grateful to you for your generosity and trust, GOD bless you abundantly and grant you may see the fruit you would wish for. I think you may.

.   .   .   .

The years 1927 and 1928 brought a great expansion in the work Father William had set himself to do. Miss Butler, the solitary to whom he had ministered at Bristol, died at the end of

1926. She left Father William money for the restoration and completion of the monastery and made him her executor and trustee. With this bequest Father William was able to restore the south side of the quadrangle, which until now had lain desolate. The pavilion at the south-east corner became a library and the rest of the south side kitchens, refectory and cells.

In any description of the monastery we must remember the buildings were originally a stable with loose horse-boxes built around three sides of a quadrangle, and a well-lighted, wide corridor to unite them under one roof. At each corner were two-storied buildings which Father William called " pavilions ". The upper storey may have been used for fodder, and the lower one as rooms for stablemen and grooms.

These horse-boxes of long-past years were changed into cells, monastic in their austerity and beautiful in their proportion; this was due to the loftiness of the buildings and large windows placed high. Whitewashed walls, a small bed, a sponge-bath and a can of water, a chair and a small chest for clothes, a holy-water stoup and a Crucifix completed the needs of a monk or a retreatant at Glasshampton.

From the open space outside these " boxes " Father William made a cloister running round the whole of the inside, and having decided that the north-west " pavilion " should be for the guests, he made a guest parlour in what originally had been a loft, and an entrance hall below. He connnected this part with the chapels by adding an additional passage, so that guests could get to the chapels without passing through the monastery, an iron grille separating the two, in this way making possible his rule that guests in a Religious House should not be free to move about with the Religious themselves. The chapel was arranged with a grille between the choir chapel for the Religious and the narthex set aside for the guests. Outside the enclosure itself, in the passage-way we have described, stands an altar for the use of visiting priests.

The whole of the interior is pure white—whitewash and white paint. No pictures were allowed except one of real distinction over the secular priests' altar. There are two or three old statues brought from Italy with their hanging lamps. Some beautiful low plaster reliefs, the work of Miss Rope the sculptress, and the gift of her niece, were at a later date let into the wall of the cloister. White curtains surround the altars, with here and there a touch of gold, and over the altar of the Blessed

Sacrament chapel a stained-glass window of adoring angels in blue and gold. In the choir chapel of our Lady, high up over the altar, is the figure of our Lord on the Cross, in memory of Harold Lloyd.

One might expect that the interior of the cells and cloisters, so devoid of colour, would be cold and repelling. It is entirely otherwise. There is a warmth and beauty and a restfulness which satisfies the soul.

Looking out, the scene is changed. Through open windows and garden doors there is a riot of colour—roses, flowering shrubs, and all kinds of rambling creepers. The green garth with its beautiful Crucifix forms three sides of a quadrangle, the fourth is open into the garden.

When the builders had finished with the house, the garden had to be created. The men with him made this their work in their hours of manual labour. The wilderness blossomed into beauty. An artist's sensibility, incessant arduous toil, the gifts of friends and, above all, the intangible alchemy which results from the energy of prayer itself, had effected a transfiguration.

He had been told that he could not make a garden on the edge of such a precipitous slope. He did his obstinate best, and never surely was there such a garden. The cottagers who found their way over these lonely fields must have been astonished to see the changed face of the building, once lying derelict, now roofed and covered with flowering creepers. In at least one of the letters that follow we have indications of his hope that the creation of a true setting for the life of prayer might do much to draw to Glasshampton those to whom God had given this vocation. Mr. Sidney King recalls an early visit to Glasshampton when Father William unfolded his dreams of the place and the gathering of twelve monks. He goes on to speak of many other visits, and how each time he found " an increasing spirit of peace upon the place ".

From among the letters of this period of reconstruction we take some written to Charles Hull, a lifelong friend of Father William. Mr. Hull, following in his father's footsteps, served as Upholsterer at Buckingham Palace. He had recently retired after executing this office in three reigns.

12 *February*, 1924.   *St. Mary at the Cross.*

    . . . It is cold and damp here but you can get about without Wellingtons. The bulbs are poking up and the birds are beginning to sing, so there is promise of the Spring, which I dearly love. Floss and cats are extraordinarily well, tho' Flossie has been in Hospital. . . .

I have a man coming to see me today from Warminster and hope he will prove to have a vocation.

I am putting all fruit under wire-netting. I don't mind the birds having a proper share, but the rascals take it *all*, so they shall have *none*. Come in the strawberry season!

31 *October*, 1925.

The old guests have gone. New ones are coming in now, as many as I can pick out. It is good the way is not my own, but I hope very much the other is to grow out of it in some way unseen.

I think Cowley and S.D.C. are getting Novices now, and I know C. R. has some, so I hope there is a stirring. I am feeling just a little of it myself. Of course there is Samuel and John Baptist and others. Parents at one time gave their children back to GOD in that way. It was perhaps rather better than our way of casting them adrift into the Sea of public school life—but there, I don't know. I am fascinated by the binding of the boy to the horns of the Altar. Anything is possible to those who love GOD. . . . Perhaps we have lost the vivid sense of a personal GOD. The Supernatural is overwhelmed by the Natural. I think too we (i.e. the world) languish for the need of real leaders. A few real prophets would assuredly thrill our poor cold souls.

I know you will pray for me and for that for which I would fain stand—faithfulness, courage and patience. . . .

I am taking a lad from Prison next week.

16 *February*, 1926.   *St. Mary at the Cross.*

A very blessed Lent to ye! . . . It is quite right you should be resting, I am sure, and enjoying your walks, and I am delighted the time does not drag heavily. . . . Go as you feel drawn, and when the lovely weather comes you may indulge in rising a little earlier *sometimes*. I think the ideal thing would be if you can elongate prayer-time sweetly and interestingly. *That* is how you will help the Church most in these days of heavy needs and grand possibilities throughout the world. *We* [1] are exempt from Fasting, but *prayer and fasting* are the things which will cast out evil and let in good. . . .

I wonder how X . . . is bearing the extra responsibility. . . . You can tell him that it is with us the " Glory of going

---

[1] At the moment of writing, both the writer and his friend were over sixty and in ill health.

on ". I would fain close my eyes to all else, for after all to indulge in hopes of growth is merely building castles in the air, and indeed it is not my business but GOD's. Of course I am only human, and I would love to have companions filling the cells, and I have my visions of the future.

I feel like Jacob. It may be that the second seven years will bring me my heart's desire. There is a little rivulet of men coming to Glasshampton from Oxford for retreat and help. Two want to spend most of the year in preparation for their Ordination in Advent. I think that is in the way of Growth. There are heaps of penitents—priests and otherwise—I could take in, but alas! we are very poor and no endowment and our Life does not appeal even to many Catholics, so we are out of the stream of benevolence. But all this is just as it should be. I can't imagine the best things flourishing easily. And that is the lesson of Lent. There must be great suffering and even death before the Triumph can be attained. . . .

7 July, 1926.

. . . My annual letter I sent you is the biggest thing I have done.[1] It looks trivial, but it cost me a great deal to write it and it answers all that has been said in *Church Times* against the Contemplative Life. I had it printed, when a most unfortunate leader appeared in *Church Times*, so I re-wrote it. I have sent out 600 mostly to Bishops and Priests and many dignitaries, including the Archbishop, who says he wants to see me! You see, my dear, we stand alone. But I think I am leavening the lump a little. At any-rate the paper carries the seed and prayer waters it—GOD must give the increase. Time flies and I have not many more years, but it would be my greatest joy to see the Life really established here for men. . . .

Tell me if you would like another book. Don't worry about too much reading. But get as much quiet time as you can alone with GOD. That is of supreme importance, especially to us older ones. We want to get to know Him or at least to be searching for HIM. " O that I knew where I might find Him "! St. Augustine says " Within you "!

My best love and GOD be gracious to you and bless you more and more. I know He will.

17 November, 1926.

We can't go at the same rate as we used to go. It is more as the Spirit drives us now. And that is better ; far. It is a terrible thing to go to the end of our days in a bustle.

[1] See p. 166.

And I trow GOD has ordained for you to go gently and beautifully. After all, it is the mind that counts. The thoughts and aspirations. The getting attuned to the State we reach hereafter. I suppose that is a state of adoring love and resting in the Lord. So I am glad for you, my dear. It is *not* laziness.

Thank you for all you are doing to broadcast the " little Papers " for me.[1] There is no hurry. I know the lack of enthusiasm and I know how difficult it is to create any interest in our Life. That is exactly why I am printing them and circulating them. It will be like sowing seeds. I try to water them with prayer. After eight years here I feel I ought to send forth some kind of message. It is opportune that it is going out now, for as you know there is a Novena of prayer for the Religious Life the last days of this month. . . .

I am just getting in estimates for finishing the Monastery, so that I can do it in bits as I can afford it. It is venturesome, but I love venture for GOD. So when you come next I hope we may perhaps be in perfect order. It will be a lovely Monastery in very lovely country and it will be the only one of strict observance for men in the Church of England. I want to leave it with a few faithful monks inside it. . . .

24 *January*, 1927.

. . . I am technically a member of S.D.C. until I have three professed, including myself. That would make a new Foundation and in the process I should automatically cease to be S.D.C. The reason of that is this. A religious cannot be cut adrift rightly, therefore in such cases as mine he must be a member of his old Community until the new one is founded. It may take fifty years to do that! I should not dream of professing anyone until I was quite certain of his stability. I would prefer to die childless.

In addition to all I have said I came away from S.D.C. with the Bishop's permission and blessing. He was Bishop Watts-Ditchfield, and he subsequently sent me a donation. Further, I did not set up an Altar until I had the Diocesan's approval of the whole venture and he (Bishop Yeatman-Biggs) blessed my Altar-Stone on the Altar of the Chapel of Lambeth Palace.

I do not think I could be more firmly and regularly Placed. Though it does not disturb me, it is a pity that anyone should cast the least reflection upon Glasshampton for his own sake.

[1] *Little Papers on the Monastic Life*, published about this time.

5 *July*, 1927.

I am so delighted you will come on July 15. . . . We shall know then more about the "Deposited Book". But it is only a phase in the long, long encounter to uphold the Catholic Faith. We have driven the enemy back a great distance since our youth and there is an increasing inrush to the Standard. My own feeling is that the Deposited Book is only another edition of the Public Worship Regulation Act. It is much better than the first edition, but it can't enforce what it aims at. It will cause us great trouble and, may be, persecutions, but the tide will flow on all the stronger the more obstructions are put up to attempt to stop it. It has always been so and it will continue so to the end.

Lord Halifax [1] is our Great Confessor. . . .

15 *February*, 1928.

Between ourselves, I was asked to preach the Three Hours on Good Friday at Graham Street, but of course refused. I don't want to injure our stand for enclosure after winning ten years to its credit. I believe *that* is what the Church of England needs as much as anything now.

We got pommelled in the gales. A huge branch of an elm was hurled on to the roof and did considerable damage.

So it is in the Spiritual Sphere. We get knocked about and bruised. . . .

My best love, and GOD grant you a very blessed Lent, my dear.

Such was the life at Glasshampton during the first decade. We see in Father William an example of something familiar to us in the lives of the Saints—a life of sacrifice which to human eyes has no apparent result. The monastery is still waiting for the men.

Father William himself lived the life there for eighteen years, and hundreds of men, both priests and lay, found in his monastery, and through him, strength to follow the way God had appointed for them, but the one supreme thing for which Father William waited and prayed was denied to him; but, as we see in these letters, whatever happened he accepted it. "It is GOD's Will, therefore it was the best thing that could have happened." He was a living witness of the reality of Dante's words in the *Paradiso*: "*In His Will is our peace*".

[1] Viscount Halifax, the father of the first Earl of Halifax, died January 19, 1934.

XI

THE EPIPHANY OF GLASSHAMPTON

Its Growing Influence and an Interruption

> True solitude is not a dream country, the refuge of disenchantment, the fatherland of obsession. It is the forgetfulness of self, but in order to find GOD and one's self. It brings into bloom the whole of that personality with which Baptism has endowed us.
>
> HUMBERT DE CLERISSAC, O.P.

A LARGE number of folk of very varying types had already begun to find at Glasshampton the peace of God. For the growth of its visible beauty had been matched and irradiated by the increasing investment of its whole life with the spirit of worship and prayer. The monastery was difficult to find the first time and always somewhat inaccessible. But the Guest-Book shows how large a proportion of visitors found something on their first visit that drew them to return.

Certain implicit principles seem to have governed the hospitality of Glasshampton. First, its host would not allow himself to do anything on his own initiative to draw people, however promising to his great purpose, to pay him a visit. He held that the contemplative can have fruitful dealings only with those whom God sends to him. More and more he sought to be hidden from the world; more and more he became conscious that the Holy Spirit Himself was causing souls characterized by certain unusual needs or by certain special gifts to find their way to the monastery. No doubt later on the number of visitors threatened to become so large as to imperil the life of solitude, silence and prayer to which he knew himself called. And in those days he did everything possible to discourage all but a few souls, men already attached to Glasshampton by ties of special intimacy, from coming to stay there. But to the very end of his time as a Solitary he showed a Christ-like incapacity to refuse certain calls.

If, despite all the precautions he had taken, by apprising his friends of his desires, to ensure hiddenness and solitude, souls in need found their way to seek his succour, he could " in no wise turn them away". The Solitary, he believed, is as common ground which no man has the ultimate right to fence away from any of God's people; for this life, as for a Devon tor or a Welsh mountain, its remoteness, its apparent bleakness and its desolation are the only final safeguards of privacy. There grew to be apparent about Father William, despite his precious gifts of understanding, friendship, sympathy and counsel, a certain majesty of soul which seemed, despite its magnetism, to claim unconsciously, and in its own right, a certain isolation. Mountain-tops are as invigorating as they are beautiful. But no man who loves them will be so lacking in sensibility as to build an hotel there.

This, however, is to look far ahead through the years. The first to come to love the transformed stables were some of its neighbours. To a few of them there is no doubt that their visits to Father William and his beneficent presence in that district made an inexpressible difference for good. Then there were some from the less immediate neighbourhood whom Providence drew this way. Hikers and others moved by curiosity about this beautiful eighteenth-century stable, standing all alone amongst trees, with the striking inscription in gold over the spandrel of the central arch, found their way within, and caught something of the generosity and large-hearted love of the Solitary who dwelt there. There was a troop of boy-scouts who came and camped close by, for whom he said Mass one morning and whose gratitude and friendship developed by frequent visits. They are commemorated by the monstrance they gave him. Soon the Birmingham leaders of this movement were to become well known to him. The Birmingham parish clergy also, priests of such a hardly tried diocese, had, he felt, a special claim upon him: he could not refuse to let them bring their men to keep a watch at the altar, and he let them take their picnic tea in the garden. Indeed, he was always willing to receive anyone who desired to be silent and pray, and on several occasions welcomed and addressed the Birmingham group of Free Catholics—a society which desired to enrich Catholicism on its historical foundations with the personal and spiritual freedom of the Protestant.

There were other groups of pilgrims quite outside the Church's boundaries. Not only could he make nonconformist visitors feel very much at home—but communists, agnostics, Jews, theosophists and free-lance individualists of diverse kinds have from time to time found here a real welcome and a disarming refusal to find in them anything but dear, though often very wayward, children of God requiring special interest and love. There were young working-men of no special religious or intellectual interests who found their way here, and who were shown round the monastery and given tea on the lawn and a straight talk afterwards. " I'm going to talk to you about Love. Now I know you all have your girls . . ." he began, and went on quite simply *via* the family to speak of the Holy Trinity.

The years after the Four Years' War had been years of great upheaval and perplexity for men who had been in the forces. Many could find no opening on returning to civilian life. And this led often as much to moral and spiritual breakdown as to economic destitution. Father William was able to give new life and hope to several such men, some of whom were in a truly desperate condition. Prison chaplains learned to commend to Father William difficult cases worthy of such a spiritual physician's generosity. He often found himself caring at one time for victims of very dissimilar afflictions. There are many priests [1] and laymen who found here moral or physical restoration and who today and always will hold his memory in gratitude. On November 18, 1930, he writes:

> Say one prayer for X . . . and Y . . ., two educated men, brothers, broken by the war and come here for healing. One rescued from the pagan Foreign Legion which he had sought to join in despair. . . . The other shattered nerves. I think they are finding the peace of GOD.

>   .   .   .   .   .

> I have another man here I should like you to meet. You might, as he is staying indefinitely. I think he is destined for a special work, and I have a dear youth who will become a postulant shortly.

>   .   .   .   .

> The Foreign Legion man is off all religion . . . and I am wooing him back. He has leave to stay as long as he likes. Y . . . has done well and found something, but it is yet a troubled face. He is helping me and may stay at least for a time. It is the war. Pray for these and others.

> I had a grateful letter from Father Z. . . . He found something too. So, without designing it, Glasshampton is a hospital.

[1] We shall speak of his work for priests under discipline in Chapter XI.

But quite apart from its work as a hospital, the monastery became increasingly a place for retreat. Its retreatants were for the most part very typical children of the English Church, and largely those who had been nourished in the Catholic tradition. Hard-worked priests who were looking for spiritual and physical refreshment and the counsel Father William could so well give, knew they would always find a welcome. Others came for more than this—for a time of refreshment in preparation for ordination or when facing problems which needed time to think out and pray over in an atmosphere of prayer. Young priests and ordinands found in Father William inspiration for their spiritual life and a standard of work which is still being lived out in many a crowded parish.

Some such men the Holy Spirit had formed into groups which gathered from time to time for re-enkindlement at St. Mary-at-the-Cross. In this way Father William's influence, wholly un-sought by himself, grew to be particularly strong with the *alumni* of two of the smaller theological colleges. Another group of young priest friends one associates particularly with the " Associa-tion for the Promotion of Retreats ". Their response to the stimulus of the vision he set before them gave him special joy; and the generosity of that response was to be by no means limited to the interior sphere. In later years the priests of his old parish, St. Peter's, Vauxhall, would come to spend some days with him. Besides these contacts with the parochial clergy, many brethren of religious communities came to visit Father William in their rest-time, and learned to look to Glasshampton for spiritual counsel and refreshment.

.   .   .   .   .   .

But to this growth of influence there came a drastic if fruitful interruption. In the autumn of 1929, Father William had a serious illness—neuritis and insomnia. He had hoped to go to St. Luke's Hostel, but his illness increased so rapidly that he was taken to the General Hospital in Birmingham.

13 *October*, 1929.   *Ward XI, General Hospital,*
                              Birmingham.

I am put in a private Ward with every attention, con-tinuously day and night. A good Chaplain and frequent Communions. Thank GOD for me. I am to have electricity for arm after rest and treatment. Still bad nights—but such a wonderful doctor [1]—one of the most brilliant in the Midlands.

17 *October.*

That was a beautiful and helpful letter you sent me. It gave me something high to aim at. It is wonderful to lie here all night awake, when the soul is resting in GOD. I can't fathom it. I can but yield to an unknown purpose.

Nurses constantly come in and look at me and make me sip hot drinks. Much twitching of legs and long spells of acute pain in arm and hand: moans and groans from those in the big Ward—that is the framework. Pray that I may learn to take and use it.

.   .   .   .

I have been under X Rays and receiving electric treatment, otherwise glued to the bed. I fancy rest and food is building up strength for Glasshampton. My doctor is strong and sure and silent.

How lovely it is to walk by faith, not to know or wish to know, tomorrow. It is so when GOD has at last disciplined the soul into the perfection of peace. Keep me well in your loving prayer.

All Souls.

I am doing well. It will take longer than I thought, but you shall hear what GOD does with me.

Early in January Father William found himself in the South of France. His doctor wanted him to escape English winds and cold, and he was sent by the kindness of friends to the Clergy Rest, *Maison de Repos*, Mentone.

The following letters were written to one of the solitaries to whom he ministered:

22 *January*, 1930.   *Maison de Repos,*
                                                    Quartier de la Madone,
                                                              Menton A.M., France.

Did you ever hear of such things? Here am I transplanted into the wealth of sunshine, blue sea and mountains. I never thought I should have to do this! . . . I manage to crawl to the R. Church to pray and be quiet. The English Church is fairly good but noisy—they are repairing the organ.

I was wafted here luxuriously by unknown friends. They lifted me from Elfinsward and put me in the train at Victoria

[1] Dr. F. W. M. Lamb, M.R.C.S., England, L.R.C.P. London, M.D. Birmingham, who remained a personal friend.

with all my tickets and passport and an envelope of French money. Cooks awaited me at Dover and placed me on board the boat. I was glad to be on the sea again. Another Cook's man seated me in a reserved sleeping-carriage in the Blue train and I went to bed, and awoke—I did not actually sleep—in the sunshine at Marseilles. From there onwards an entrancing panorama of seascape, blue sea, and mountains and here I am, rather feeble but, I think, feeling the healing going on.

10 *February.*   *Maison de Repos, Menton.*

I have had much of von Hügel recurring to me here. I think I can detect the power of the unchanging stability of the R.C. It carries the people along with it. There are, I know, defects and weaknesses, but they are hidden and unseen. I met a company of Seminary boys out for exercise in Italy. I confess it thrilled me. It was like a witness to the world of gaiety, of the age-long flow of the supernatural—their cassocks speak of the fact that they are " slightly reverend ". I think we are regaining that at, for instance, Kelham. A friend drove me up to Gorbio—a village hanging to the side of a mountain—very ancient and quaint. I caught sight of the Curé teaching the children the Catechism in the bright and homely Church. One little mite in disgrace kneeling out in the centre. How that peep seemed to sanctify all the lovely village! All the world over it is the same. In the mind of GOD there is but one Mystical Body. The fierce controversies and the wicked divisions are only on the surface as the result of man's perversity and pride. Like all sin, it is distressing and must be repented of, but even in this perplexing age there are undoubted indications of the Loving Providence ordering good out of evil and it is fraught with promising and immense possibilities. Our contribution lies in the hidden recesses of prayer and in fidelity to the Sacred Heart. I found myself opposite the Altar of Our Lady of Sorrows in the Church at Mass on Sunday and felt at home.

It is a long exile—albeit in the Sun. Perhaps I may return to the second phase and be permitted to witness others doing what has been denied me. Who can tell? I never for a moment realized I was destined to such an extended and varied digression when I left Glasshampton early in October for the hospital at Birmingham with a small handbag, expecting to return in a week or so, my body mended. . . .

We have it wet and cold, but I *am* healing slowly, and try to be submissive to the Sacramental means of full recovery, resting much upon your prayer.

11 *March*, 1930.   *Maison de Repos,*
                                      Quartier de la Madone,
                                      Menton A.M.

I was so glad to get your letter and to know how you have welcomed Lent. . . . I agree with you absolutely about the ordering of the Divine Office.   Though I am well acquainted with the humiliating feeling of being unable for the moment to touch the exact perfection of time which seems to fit the purpose in the mind of the Church.   I think we must be *quick to offer the humiliation,* and just ask for strength to enable us to press on.   I say " press on ", but not so much to the perfected method as to the tranquillity that can somehow give the fullness of praise and adoration by means of a restricted rule.   So " press on." . . .

Whatever happens, don't yield to getting *vexed* with yourself!   That is worse than failure!   Instead, the failure should be offered with yourself inside it.   Then there will be no break or jerk.   I hope you can see what I mean.   It is this : as we co-operate with Grace and notice, more and more, our personal failures, we are to learn to let nothing disturb the pure desire so wonderfully implanted in our hearts.   If there is nothing but failure, be humble enough to offer *that* ; if it is all we have to offer, it is ourselves.   That applies to the whole of life, and there is nothing else that can give us such inspiration and reality.   Having made the complete oblation of the whole self to GOD for ever, *all* we do is filled out with love ;   henceforth and forevermore we are His.

.   .   .   .   .   .

I am decidedly better.   It was unfortunate weather in February.   I hope the real Riviera weather has arrived.   I am advised to stay on as long as possible.   That may be end of April.   It seems right to get as well as I can. . . . I can use my hand and arm and write better, but not for long at a stretch.

3 *April*, 1930.

It was Refreshment Sunday and I heard Vespers in the R.C. Cathedral, Nice.   It was packed and there were at least six groups of different Communities of Sisters.   A Franciscan preached. . . . I went on to Cannes to catch the steamer next morning to the Isle of Lerins.   I was agreeably surprised to find there a Monastery with thirty Cistercian Monks. One Brother explained to me that Clemenceau used his influence on their behalf and so they were not expelled as had been the Carthusians from Grande Chartreuse.   It was a delightful trip on the sea in the sun, and the loveliness of the islands indescribable.   The silence and order of the Monastery seemed exactly the right use of it all. . . .

The Dr. says there is some strain of heart and blood pressure and he has ordered massage for arm and hand. But I am infinitely better, thank GOD, though I think I have to stay till they close down on May 1st.

23 April, 1930.

I was so glad to hear from you for Easter.   I missed the order and quiet of the Monastery and I could not have the Passiontide and Easter I could have wished.   I said the Divine Office alone in my room—it was more help to me than attending when said in the Latin tongue.   I was at High Mass at Sacré Coeur on Palm Sunday.   It was thronged and crowds standing—a great number of children with palms decorated with chocolates and other dainties! (a local custom I believe!). . . . If they had shouted out " Hosannah to the Son of David " it would have added greatly to the joy, but they sang nothing.   I was able to say Mass at 7 on Easter Day, and I was at Sacré Coeur again for some time in the afternoon watching the poor people coming in and out to say their devotions and I stayed on for Vespers and Benediction. . . . I am going to the Isle of Lerins for a short Retreat with the Cistercians in their Abbey when I leave here.

April 25, 1930.

It is very good of you to allow me to know the innermost movements of your soul—how it has lingered over the Way of the Cross ever since Easter.   I had that experience too!

I wonder sometimes that we can so quickly pass through the re-presentation of the Passion.   It is rather like the way the cars tear through all this magnificent mountain scenery. I want to get out and sit down and drink in one part of it, but then I must needs take my tent and dwell in the midst of it all the days of my life, for is it not inexhaustible?

Perhaps that is what we are for—Set aside to glorify the Saviour by *prolonged* contemplation of eternal mysteries.   But how it leaves one prostrate in utter nothingness!!

I sat all Easter afternoon in Sacré Coeur and watched the *poor* come in—they mostly lingered at the Chapel of Our Lady of Sorrows—women (with no head-dress!) with little children—and hard-worked men all kneeling still for long stretches of time—they too were lingering in Holy Week. Then we all gathered together for Vespers and Benediction. I think we were exactly as you were.   And it is so good to hold up the *healed* scars of our souls to the Risen Jesus.   Truly an Easter Triumph.

I leave May 1 for Cannes and cross to the Isle of Lerins to make a short retreat of three days in the Cistercian Abbey, and what can my retreat be but the same lingering? I may get out at Marseilles to say a prayer over the spot where Cassian built his monastery. Thence to Avignon and to stop a few days in an Inn in the woods about a mile from Grande Chartreuse in order to linger about holy ground.

2 *May*, 1930.   *The Abbey, S. Honoret,*
                                                         Isle of Lerins.

                        To Charles Hull.

I am really coming home by easy stages, so please don't be alarmed.

I have come here for a little retreat, and they are most kind and hospitable. I am very glad to be thrown among Brethren of other obedience, and I am more than ever persuaded that we are *one*. All have their characteristic excellencies, and when we are *officially* knit together we shall make a much more formidable front towards the enemy.

I shall get out to say a prayer over the site of Cassian's Monastery at Marseilles and take a peep at Avignon and pilgrimage from Grenoble to La Grande Chartreuse. I hope to arrive at Victoria at 7.15 p.m. on Sunday. I am very sorry it is Sunday, but it is difficult to avoid this journey.

.   .   .   .   .   .

The Wind is up. It is like Patmos. Everywhere on the island you can hear the sea breaking on the surrounding rocks like " the voice of many waters ".

To his sister he had written on Lady Day:

I went to Nice to see the Abbé Nartus, whom I knew when at Westminster Cathedral. Very nice and shewed me about. He lives alone like a hermit. He made me some tea.

And again on May 13 after reaching England:

I hit upon the 500th anniversary of the Martyrdom of St. Joan of Arc in Paris. Heard Mass at the Madeleine and stood for some hours on the steps outside watching the unending procession of Guilds of men and boys marching with wreaths to place at the Saint's statue. There must have been thousands upon thousands with banners and bands . . . and all with their priests. I never saw such a sight. One felt they had all made their confessions and communions—a thrilling witness to Holy Religion.

28 *May*, 1930.   *St. Mary at the Cross.*
                        To Charles Hull.

Here I am, you see.   Dear old England! there is no place so lovely.

I don't think the monks at Lerins quite made me out, but they were good, and the old Guest-Master kissed me when I left. . . .

You will be interested to hear that I thought I would peep into the Casino at Monte Carlo just to see with my own eyes. But when I presented myself they politely refused me admisson as being an undesirable person.   I am rather proud of that! Of course I wore my habit.

Avignon is grand, but has no Christian atmosphere.   La Grande Chartreuse in its desolation almost made me weep. It is in a wonderful place among the mountains.[1] . . .

My little book *Mysteries of the Incarnate Life* is in the Press at S.P.C.K. 1/-.

And—it is the greatest joy to be in the Monastery again and able to go to the Altar each morning.

Then follow letters to various people:

May 1930.

I came home to the singing of birds and in a gleam of sunshine.   There is the inevitable pile of letters and there is a great deal to get in order after so long an absence.

Then I must write and send round an " encyclical " to all our friends to say I am alive.

.   .   .   .   .   .

We shall soon be smothered in roses here.   All the decorations are round the outside.   I never cut them to bring them in.

.   .   .   .   .   .

Please pray much for guidance in drawing up some deed to ensure continuity here.   I am sure it is to be, but all the more reason for it to be spread out before God.

On receiving a gift towards his work Father William writes:

It will help towards the Guest House, which I must soon face if postulants come and stay.   Then all guests will be shut out of the Monastery proper except the Narthex.   The walls and roof are here—it is the only bit of the old Stable I have not converted and adjoins the kitchen from which we can easily send their food.   I fear it will cost some hundreds

[1] The monks of La Grande Chartreuse were allowed to return to the Monastery in 1940.

to do but, as before, the Holy Angels will bring what is necessary.

. . . . . .

That touch with the world through letter-writing is all to the good so long as it *comes* to us—even better than interviews in these days, I think. It is *my* chief work now.

Please pray for a priest who seeks to test his vocation. It would mean so much for this place if he found it here.

I had the Birmingham F.C.P. priests on S. John Baptist and did too much! but recovered.

8 July.

I forget if I asked your prayers for the negotiations going on between me and a company of Priests in view of securing continuity here in the event of my early death—it will secure the Monastery in a way agreeable to the landlord, who wants it to be given to GOD in perpetuity.

August 1930.

My *Little Papers on the Monastic Life* [1] are appearing as leading articles in the S.S.J.E. Canadian Magazine— anonymously, of course. It is very pleasant to feel such scraps should be so used. I had dared to hope they might have found circulation in England. But England and the C. of E. is too busy with other things!

Feast of St. Michael and All Angels, 1930.

I am distressed for the unemployed. I dream of someone laying hold of them to do *voluntary* work for GOD and humanity and so to turn the edge of the demoralizing and drab dole. It looks to me as if the revolt is not so much against organized religion as against the inconsistency of the lives of those who preach it, and that perhaps evangelists with no possessions, shorn even of all ecclesiasticism (tho' not of the Faith), would give to the Christian Religion an untrammelled channel of expression which would make its appeal as it did through the disciples of our Lord and as He set them the example.

You will retort, "Why don't you go yourself?" My answer, "Because Our Lord said, ' *Pray* ye the Lord of the harvest that He will send, etc.' " Perhaps the shortage of evangelists arises from the fact that there are so few praying? Our work here is to pray.

It is a great joy to me to know enthusiastic apostolic friends at whom I may cast my pellets!

[1] These were afterwards incorporated into the *Blossoming of the Desert*, A. R. Mowbray and Co., 1931.

6 *October*, 1930.

I had fourteen young men in the Narthex yesterday. They had bicycled over from Birmingham. They go out like that every Sunday, and I doubt if they ever go to Church. They have good faces and they sang and prayed so nicely. When they heard I was in Hospital last year they made a collection and sent it to me. *Of course* they are full of religion, but somehow they are alienated from GOD's Church. The Pharisee misses all that splendid material and so does ecclesiasticism. S. Francis got behind all the mere formality and reached the souls of the people, as did our Blessed Lord Himself. The externals are all right if they spring out of interior love and devotion.

17 *December*, 1930.

Last Christmas I was away and the Christmas before quite alone, so indeed I have a very great deal to be most thankful for. . . .

I get rather to like disappointments and delays. How much sweeter they make the fullness of blessing when it comes!

27 *December*, 1930.   *North Pole*.

We have been in the Arctic regions up here, and I daresay you have snow too.

The Bambino lies on the straw in the Stable in the midst of the Chapel—in the place of a lectern—and we knelt there together after the first Mass at Midnight in the wonderful stillness of the Park. Just a few of us—one newly made Postulant.

28 *January*, 1931.

I will tell you some of the wonderful happenings hereabouts. A young man came driven by the Spirit from the Bull Ring, Birmingham. A roughish lad but so simple and direct. He has simply been hungry for GOD, and was in utter confusion as to where to go and to what to attach himself. Somehow he got here and the light blazed in upon him in the quiet of the Chapel. I sent him to a priest in Birmingham to be instructed for Confirmation, but he comes here for week-ends. He loves solitude and prayer and offers himself to GOD in this life.

It came to me a week or so ago that the last ray of hope for Glasshampton was flickering out when I was taken to Hospital and some thought I should never return. Since GOD brought me back. . . . I have thought, the desert is surely blossoming? And that led me to gather up my Little Papers and re-arrange them and lo! and behold!

a new book is typed, *The Blossoming of the Desert*. It won't seem much to you, I fear, but to me it is a great deal. In a small compass it is a sort of miniature of my experiences.

And I was led to ask the Archbishop of York [1] if I might write to him about fallen priests. . . . He gave me permission, and a long letter has gone to him. Will you say one prayer that he may be led to do something?

That is all. These happenings have helped me tremendously and I feel there is a true stirring.

And there is one more I forgot. The Bishop of X . . . has directed a would-be Anchoress to me. I think it is a great wonder for a Bishop to do that! I know you will understand my joy that after twelve years there is evidently some stirring of the waters.

10 *February*, 1931. *S. Scholastica's Day.*

I can hear the black-bird singing—full of promise.

23 *February*.

Unless some saint like S. Scholastica discerns the possibilities, or of course GOD Himself, that bit of the Stable will remain derelict for another twelve years. But we shall know it is quite as it should be, though my frailty dreams dreams!

It was after his recovery in the South of France and return to Glasshampton that the desert blossomed for Father William. Not that he was ever able to fulfil his aim of founding a Contemplative Community, though a constant stream of promising postulants flowed in and out of the Monastery. It may well have been in part that the other stream of guests that mingled with it prevented it settling into still waters. But the Father's generosity was also in part to blame. He would send a promising inmate away to the Cowley Fathers or Nashdom that they might see what community life with others was really like, as they could not living alone with him at Glasshampton, and he would give them fullest encouragement to stay there if they wished.

Father William himself wrote:

25 *June*, 1931.

I feel now that I have given up the hope of companions—or of a Foundation—I am happier. If GOD sent two or three good priests I should know He meant *them* to " found ".

.   .   .   .   .   .

[1] Then His Grace the Right Reverend William Temple, D.D.

Glasshampton is waiting for priests. I don't say GOD will ever give them. But I can see clearly I must shut down the novitiate and greatly reduce the retreatants unless priests come. That is what GOD seems to ask for at the moment, by the fourteen years barrenness. I can offer it and wait. I shall rejoice equally either way. I can indeed try my best as a solitary, or I can stand aside and delight in seeing others enter in to build up according to His Will.

15 August, 1931.

It is quite evident I am not to escape being a Solitary, and I am waiting to learn exactly how it is to be done. You say Glasshampton is to stand. I believe you. Yet I must watch to secure its continuity in character, that it does not become another centre of violent activity. It might easily do that.

11 September, 1931.

My Arab of the desert and of caves has lingered out the week. He spends hours before the Blessed Sacrament. He is unorthodox but has devoured *Cassian* and *Charles de Foucauld* and has returned to Communion. He is Eton and Cambridge and has aristocratic connections. Certainly his prayer and silence are quite unique. He wears a sort of cowl and looks very Eastern.

7 November, 1931.

Did you ever read the life of Bishop Collins? Very brilliant and a great saint, but breathless. He was a friend of mine, and I have just read his *Life* again, he makes me feel a worm—but I can't help feeling GOD never meant us to go at that pace. At anyrate few can do it and save their own souls. I feel where there is such fever prevalent there is the greater need of the prayer life—but I doubt if they can profitably mix together.

23 February, 1932.

I have been asked to act as Extraordinary Confessor to an enclosed Community, and I must go four times a year. They are enclosed, so I may accept them. I only go out to those who are. That is *my* work. My grief is that there are no men anywhere enclosed.

8 March, 1932.

I have just re-read the Baron's *Letters to his Niece*. They ought to have done me good. Yes, he and Newman are great souls, and so is Gore.

I hope you keep well. I think you will if you secure sufficient time to be quiet. How the Baron had to save up his energy!

Monday in Holy Week, 1932.

We need a crusade against the general standard of clerical life—quite as much as that first Tract of Newman's was needed—ease, comfort and self-indulgence. . . .

Just think! At a big Mission in London there were rows of unemployed men every night. Afterwards they slept on the Embankment, and the others all went home to their warm beds. . . .

There is a group of (these men) at Vauxhall, where X . . . is this week. I have sent an emissary this morning to see if I can get some of them here. . . . After all, St. Francis was right—give all and ask for nothing. It is the right way for the ambassador of the Crucified, and nothing else can be expected to appeal to the human heart.

Forgive my intrusion (on Holy Week).

Easter Tuesday, 1932.

Such invasions yesterday. One dear man with a boy—a sweet lad, but not brilliant. The father is at Mass every morning before business.

Two men—father and son—are coming into Retreat soon. And several others I think I might rightly encourage to come, but dare I? I would not hesitate if I had a priest-companion, but it seems wrong with only my broken self.

Do pray that I may be guided to do what is right. I can place them elsewhere. . . . We do want to see Cowley fed and nourished : I could point them that way.

So I wait for GOD's sign.

19 *April,* 1932.

I think I am the hindrance to growth here. Just now there are four more or less promising. I have asked X . . . to go as guest to Cowley for a week and talk to Father Y . . ., but he seems to want to come here. If he does come I think we shall veer towards Carthusianism. At anyrate I want GOD to form the life by those He sends.

21 *May,* 1932.

Such happenings still going on! I think the Carthusian will come home in July and there is another Carthusian retreating, a B.Sc. He came two years ago and rather drifted, but is again stirred, and it looks as tho' he will succumb to Whitsun.

A boy of eighteen was here from Sunday evening to Tuesday, and evidently looked wistfully at the life and went away wondering.

Another of eighteen rang the bell on Monday, a Rover from Birmingham. He had heard of and is coming to one of the week-end encampments here, but bicycled over to enquire about a longer retreat for himself. He told me how he had passed from chapel to low Church and then to catholicism. Old for his years and I should think clever. He will come in retreat. . . .

I am going to send out a leaflet to all my friends and to the S.S.C. (200 priests). It may move priests to take some interest in the Religious Life. Mowbray's paper goes to the Priests Convention in Oxford in July, also to centenary next year.

.   .   .   .   .   .

India thrills me. There is such danger, but such magnificent opportunities. I am sorry Lord Irwin is not on the spot. But he is working and praying. Read the Pope's Encyclical.

Feast of SS. Peter and Paul, June 29, 1932.

A deputation of Cambridge men waited on me and followed it up with an invitation from Fr. Milner White to address S.T.C. in Autumn on the Contemplative Life. I replied that my very presence would contradict some important points I should wish to emphasize. He answers that he understands completely.

But it was a great temptation!

9 July, 1932.

It is a blessed joy to have Oblates or close associates like X. and Y. and Z. That gives hope for the future when I am called away. And it is better thus than a houseful of monks with not the right spirit of humble and holy prayer and mortification to hold them together, and GOD can raise up such at any moment.

And what better than to abide His time?

As I said, after my obligations this summer and autumn, I intend to shut the door and devote all energies to my own life and that of recluses and nuns only.

7 August, 1932.

Do these men realize the days that are coming upon us? Have they their eyes upon the world-wide threatenings of a universal collapse in the breaking up of the present civilization? With it is likely to come the dis-establishment of the C. of E., and then there will be real poverty for the clergy and sifting of men, and only those really disciplined and ready for it will be able to contribute to the new and, please GOD, better order of things.

I was greatly stirred by the Conference last week, and it set me searching into where I stand and caused me to surrender even Glasshampton.

I knew I must test my detachment and hold myself ready to do anything in response to what we all recognized as a very loud call of GOD. For days it kept me sitting loosely to what I most cherish, in order to go into the midst of the famished, and share *their* life for the love of GOD, and of these His children.

The answer has come that I must stay where I am. It came to me direct from GOD, and also through those I submitted it to. But it means some *re-ordering* of my life, necessitating the closing of the door to guests until GOD gives me a Guest-House and a companion or two to carry out, according to His showing, the twofold ideal of silence and prayer, and of ministering hospitality to those He sends us. That clearly is the only reason I am to continue at Glasshampton. Further than that I cannot see.

The Guest-House was never given. But even through the years of solitude that followed, God rendered possible, now in one way, now in another, the carrying out of the " twofold ideal ". Father William continued to minister to those whom he recognized as sent by the Holy Ghost.

The impressions of one thus favoured, a distinguished priest-theologian of the Eastern Orthodox Church, formerly a priest of the Roman Catholic Church, will fittingly close this chapter.

Father Lev Gillet writes:

J'ai passé une semaine à St. Mary at the Cross en août 1935. Je n'ai parlé à Fr. William que deux fois, lors de mon arrivée et lors de mon départ. Je lui ai demandé de me permettre de garder le silence tout le reste du temps. Il y a eu pendant quelques jours un ' clergyman '; une fois deux ' boy scouts ' sont venus en visite. J'ai été très impressioné par la pieté et le rayonnement de Fr. W. Quand il chantait seul dans sa chapelle, son corps se soulevait et semblait prendre un élan en haut. Je me rapelle une scène étrange: un jour Fr. W. célébrait à l'autel, de grand matin, et le chat était à côté de lui *debout* sur ses pattes de derrière et s'appuyant avec les pattes de devant sur l'antependium (frontal?). J'ai pensé à une page des " Fioretti ". Je voulais aider Fr. W.

à laver la vaisselle, mais il refusa avec un sourire charmant, et me dit à l'oreille : " the fairies are doing it ".

Il me dit aussi qu'il ne voulait pas enlever le miel à ses abeilles. Encore les " Fioretti ". Dans notre dernière conversation il m'a parlé des difficultés de la position anglicane : (" There is nothing so difficult as being an Anglican "). Il m'a dit sa tristesse de voir que personne ne se joignait à lui dans son monastère. Il m'a positivement offert son monastère si je pouvais trouver des Russes qui voudraient y vivre une vie contemplative. Depuis j'ai toujours le regret qu'un petit monastère " oecuménique " anglo-russe n'a pas pu continuer la tradition de Fr. W. Il m'a aussi raconté qu'une fois invité à prêcher dans une " cathedral town " il est allé voir l'evêque. " I told him ' Father—yes, I shall call you " Father ", not " my Lord ", things are very bad in your diocese. It's not preaching you need here, it's praying and fasting.' The Bishop was at first very angry, but afterwards it was all right." Fr. W. est un des deux ou trois personnes qui m'ont donné une vive impression de sainteté. Il m'a semblé être une combinaison de la sainteté carthusienne et de la sainteté franciscaine. J'ai emporté de St. Mary at the Cross une vision de lumière et de joie.

PART IV

SOLITARY

XII

THE FRUITS OF SOLITUDE

A few such secret and unknown servants of God are the chariots and horse-men, the strength and bulwarks of the kingdoms and churches where they live.
AUGUSTINE BAKER, *Sancta Sophia.*

THE brightness of the beginning of Glasshampton and of the years which followed ended, as we have seen, under the shadow of the Cross. Companions upon whom Father William had set great store left him, and he passed through a phase of great darkness, in which, however, he could still hold and accept the Will of God. When it was clear to him that it was the Will of God, he sent men, both priests and lay, to other communities and lived quietly his own life of prayer, always within it an ever-deepening note of reparation for sin, as he had seen and ministered to it in the world.

When he was left quite alone one year on December 31 he writes:

> I know how good it is if GOD breaks up all one's plans. One can so easily do the best things and yet not be in the way of His Will. One can be *alongside* of His Will but *outside*. Will you thank God for me that He gives me grace to welcome even failure, if it is His Will? Indeed, I have frequently told Him so in my prayer.

And alone in his monastery, hidden in the great park, he sets up the Crib, the wreath and the evergreens: "It is very beautiful," he writes; "I try to live the life in its fullness."

He felt more than ever that the enclosed life for men was the greatest need of the Church of England. Even in the midst of his own failure to have founded such a community he could write:

> I am persuaded GOD wants it. Being where I am and having come to it as I did, I must stand by it, even if I die

alone, I can only go on trying to do my best. The rest is not my responsibility, but HIS. That is what I believe with my whole soul.

But the reader will be better able to judge from the complete letter:

31 *December*.

I knew you would give me your sympathy and love, and advice too, though I felt keenly having to tell you and to bring a little shadow into your rejoicings. I can only spread it out before GOD. If I can look up I am of course quite happy whatever happens, and the way I am in can only be true with its trials and sufferings.

They surely make it true if lovingly embraced. One's poor human frailty feels bruised, but that is just it, and without those experiences what is there to offer?

So that is what I am trying to do. There is gladness in having to go through the deep waters. GOD has been so good to me, and it is true to say that I am sometimes terrified at freedom from suffering.

I think one is drawn nearer to our LORD when alone, and I am trying to gather up the blessings I am surrounded with.

And I gently clean the place and cook, and for the rest I pray and read. It is really most beautiful. I suppose the pain of it is in *self*, but then I know how good it is if GOD breaks up all one's plans. One can so easily do the best things and yet not be in the way of His Will. You can be *alongside* His Will, but *outside*.

So I must be quiet and draw nearer to Him, and submit myself to Him, and wait till He shews. It may be the end, I can't say. I must just try to be the prisoner of the LORD. I read somewhere lately another description, and I like it better—" Shut up in GOD's birdcage ".

There is no news from B . . ., and I do not expect him back, and I would not have any pressure put upon him to come back. He mentioned among other things his call to the priesthood and no Sung Mass. It was his failure to pass his exams that brought him here. His quietness and prayer and his work were all good, and gave me great hopes.

The root of the difficulty is not only the dearth of vocation, but the inability to embrace it. And that throws us back upon GOD Himself.

My coming out of S.D.C. was for myself first. The whole difficulty all along was to come alone, and it was only at the end . . . that S.D.C. yielded to my request. And I remember my own words in my last appeal were, that whether others joined me or not, must be left to GOD. And that is where I stand at the end of ten years.

And shall we be right to be disappointed or surprised? Is it not a tremendous thing to ask a man to do, especially in these days? Even if I were a saint and all were perfectly ordered. Even then it is a very great deal to expect of *men*.

No! I shan't eat my heart out. That would be sad. I think there is something to rise up to, and it is a great joy to have the blessed privilege of trying to live the life myself alone.

Besides, we ask for GOD's Will to be done. We must not rejoice less if, when He grants it, it appears in the form of failure rather than success. I say failure, but it can't be that if I am faithful, and you know I shall always remain hopeful; even now there is a feeling men with vocation will be raised up ere long.

When I get time I shall turn to trying to write the other papers.

Now, thank you for your letters. Try to rejoice with me at this answer to the surrender of it all into GOD's Hands. Only pray that I may be true and humble and learn my lesson.

And will you thank GOD for me that He gives me grace to welcome even failure—if it is His Will—indeed, I have frequently told Him so in my prayer.

I hope all are well and happy. I must " sit on the nest ", as Father Andrew said, but I would so have liked to be able to come.

GOD bless you all and my love.

Yours ever affectionately and gratefully,

WILLIAM.

I set up the Crib and the wreath and evergreens and it is very beautiful and I try to live the Life in its fullness.

The solitary life had begun. Priests and penitents came to make their souls, but he did not again receive postulants definitely for the Religious Life at Glasshampton. He would have done so if he had had a Priest-Religious professed with him, but he did not think it right, after he was seventy years old, to receive a layman with a view to profession, however clearly marked his vocation:

Lady Day, 1933.

If any come to me with probable vocation I must continue to send them to Cowley or Nashdom. I have up to now hoped that one or two priests with vocation might come, but now I can see it is very unlikely, and I must act accordingly. I do want you thoroughly to grasp my precarious position. I think my feeble witness will end as a Solitary.

.   .   .   .   .   .

I should so enjoy the School! Father Benson once said we should " enter an Infants School as into a Community of Saints ! "

On November 16, 1934, he wrote to Charles Hull:

. . . It will take a long time to create the right atmosphere in the C. of E. such as will give birth to the spirit of martyrdom. It seems to me it is too dense to allow all that has been said and written to penetrate—Benson, Gore, etc. We are choked! And their great books are shelved and dusty. Nothing else than an increased body of men living *out* all that literally, will clear the atmosphere—for which we must pray. But I do feel very strongly that the great mass of people never get hold of the right teaching. They can't afford the books that contain it. And *there* is what must be drawn upon, I think, for heroism.

. . . You know I am a veritable hermit now. I can't tell you of the peace it is and how one seems able to get through to GOD in a new way. I had not fully realized the strain of those sixteen years with more or less unwilling horses to drive all the time. . . .

21 *December*, 1934.

I remember my first Midnight Mass. I went from Highgate to St. Albans, Holborn, and Father Stanton was there. It was a magnificent service, and I was deeply impressed. I had never before so vividly realized the Nativity as at the moment of the Consecration at the very time of His birth. . . .

Yes, I am alone, and it is very sweet and blessed. I could not have planned it so, but it is His gift to me, and I thank Him for it.

I am enjoying working on a small pamphlet entitled *Achievement*, following up *Blossoming*. Dom Bernard is to write a few words of preface. But it won't be published till the Spring. It is not only to Youth, but to priests and Bishops.

About this time he was asked to undertake the direction of several solitaries, work for which he was admirably fitted, and which he had been doing since he went to Bristol in 1912. This was one of the two calls which took him away from Glasshampton; the other was in connection with his duties as Extra-Confessor to communities of nuns, " They are enclosed. I only go out to such now. That is my work." And the reader will remember his humble surprise when a Bishop asked him to undertake the direction of a Solitary: " I think it is a great wonder for a Bishop to do that! "

We are not concerned at the moment as to whether or no the solitary life has rightly a place in the Church. Father William accepted it where he found it, and with great gladness and understanding, but he was not responsible for its initiation.

We believe that the late Archbishop Temple [1] had been asked to recognize and give permission for such a life, which was common both for anchorets and anchoresses in the early Church and existed in England down to the Reformation. The Church of Rome does not recognize these as " Religious " where the condition of common life is wanting. The Church of England is less exclusive in its recognition of them. But where this life can be lived under the shelter of a Religious House, and perhaps best of all by one who for some years has lived the Religious Life in Community, it has special promise of permanency, and is safeguarded against the danger of unreality. To those whom Father William found already established in this way he gladly gave care and direction. And he clearly well understood the point of view taken in the revised Canon law of the Roman church. [2] But he would not try to anticipate the action of Providence.

He wrote:

> I do think it would be an immense help to solitaries— and to the Church at large—if they were in *groups*. Not interfering with each other's rules and not ordinarily meeting one another. But *all* attend Mass together. But I should not manufacture it. It must come of GOD.

In September, 1935, Father William had again to go to the General Hospital, Birmingham, for treatment. He writes:

> 26 *September*, 1935.
>
> I am glad to be back. It is a great experience. The Hospital is one of the real power-centres.
>
> To see the Ward full of wee babies in deep silence. To stand in the room where they are all born. To be in the Chapel and in the prayer corner or in the garden was a series of wonders and privileges. They were all so kind, and truly it was among old friends I found myself.

[1] Then Archbishop of York 1929–42. Later Archbishop of Canterbury, died October 26, 1944.
[2] The new Canon law, Canon 487.

The Rev. Sydney King tells us that " on this visit, as on his first stay in the Hospital, Father William easily became a source of attraction to doctors, nurses and patients. On one occasion the Navvy Missioner approached him—wrapt up in bed—and spoke to him about God and his soul, not knowing to whom he was talking. Father William listened with very great interest and kindliness. Then he thanked the Missioner and said, ' Yes! all that you say is very, very good and when I go back to the Monastery I will show you something of the Catholic Faith! '

" In his convalescent garb he took his place with the men patients who were allowed to move about in the wards and listened to their talk. He was surprised to find how discontented they all seemed, doubting everybody's motives of goodness and honesty. Once they asked him what *he* thought, and then he told them of his poverty ' for the Love of God, to win men to peace and happiness through Jesus Christ.'

" On this last visit to the Hospital, I gave him a little statue of St. Francis, but by the next time I went, it had gone—' You see I went into the other Ward and had a talk with a boy there, so I gave it to him.' "

But the Solitary was not idle. It was during these years when Father William was left alone, so far as companions in the monastic life were concerned, that he realized his great longing to help priests who had fallen by the way. He had always been much occupied and distressed by the number of priests with whom he came in contact who, through moral failure, or never having fully understood the obligations of the priestly life, or been rightly prepared for it, were under ecclesiastical discipline and forbidden to exercise their ministry or had no desire to do so.

Bishops and priests came to know that Father William would not refuse to help such cases, and these outcasts from society found their way to the Solitary at Glasshampton, knowing that whatever confidence they gave him, or in whatever form, it would be preserved inviolate. How many he helped back to the way of penitence is known only to GOD, for by its very nature this is a work which must be hidden and unknown. To an old friend to whom he had written for material help to meet such cases he wrote:

Thank you a thousand times over for your kindest of letters. It *does* ease my mind a lot, and I will not take advantage of it, but pay up as quickly as I am able. The fact is for nearly a year now I have had these impecunious guests sent by Bishops and others. I tried to refuse each time, but it seemed like kicking against the pricks. It is a work greatly needed in the Church of England, and one which Contemplatives can very well do as at Mt. Mellaray in Ireland. I have seen my Bishop about it. I know Father Adderley feels the need of such a place, so you may mention it to him as being an additional burden laid on me, but otherwise please keep it hidden, as the " *hiddenness* " is part of the treatment. It is an anxiety spiritually and pecuniarily, but perhaps someone may be raised up to help me through. I am praying for that in a Novena now going on with us. I feel it may be GOD's Will to use us in this way, especially as it came quite unexpectedly and unsought. But you can realize the additional expense it means and the work, and you will realize, too, that the furniture has been in good use. Say an *Our Father* for the Novena, will you? When you come I will tell you a little about these poor men. . . . The problem is to keep them quite separate from those who come to live the Life. I could do that nicely if only I could complete the monastery.

But all this is selfish about my own affairs. It is only revealed to you that you may know better my difficulties and the need I am in of substantial help. I *can* only get it privately, as I am determined never to appeal publicly for ourselves, and certainly not for this little work for GOD's priests. Isn't it a work of Divine Compassion? . . .

Flossie's hair has come off! I am treating her for a new coat in the spring. The two pussies are perfectly beautiful. They all three follow me round when I garden. My grateful love. . . .

To the same friend of his youth he wrote later:

There are no vocations, but I seem to feel there is a stirring in this direction, from letters I receive. I have had a continuous flow of Priest-penitents in the Guest House, and Bishops and others still write and ask me to take more. I think this is GOD's way of bringing them to recognize the great need there is of such Houses as this. If one can only live long enough and hold on in patience and faithfulness, and not despise the day of small things, all will be well. As Father Newland-Smith wrote to me, " The Contemplative Life is bound to come sooner or later and pioneers must stand alone ". That was a word of fine wisdom and encouragement, and stands in great contrast to the preaching and writing of Canon X . . .—but he always did lag behind, poor dear.

How I wish you lived near here, that you could . . . take part in our three Christmas Masses and visits to the Blessed Crib. Like you, I am entranced by the Nativity, and always was as a boy even, when we used to gather in the Schools at Christ Church on Christmas morning to sing Carols!

To a priest entering upon a Chaplaincy to a Religious House:

A brief greeting on your settling in with the Sisters and to beg your prayers for,

1. X . . ., who I am taking in from Embankment, filthy and in rags—educated, but lost and in deep debt.
2. Y . . ., the Welsh recluse in Retreat here.
3. Z . . ., a new deacon retreating here before starting his work.
4. Twenty men from Birmingham, Quiet Day 21st.
5. W . . ., a priest coming for re-kindlement.

Then spread out before GOD for me this house and what is its very pressing need—viz., to make the lumber-end into a new separate Guest-House. It would cost £1000, but it would keep all guests out of the Monastery and give us less disturbance and more quiet and seclusion. As you know, we never " appeal " and never know publicity—GOD always sends what we need, but it is our duty to ask Him. We have just spent £100 on repairs, etc., and I am bound to spend another £159 at once on rectifying the ineffectual heating apparatus. I am only doing so after consulting two independent experts, and they exactly agree. So our " nest-egg " disappears. I have no fears or anxieties, but we need plenty of prayer.

I should so plan the Guest House that we could begin there the work for our brethren who are broken one way or another. I don't think it would be good to have many such *together*— but it would be as GOD guided. The need is really pressing unless we close the doors to them.[1]

Dear as this work was to Father William's heart, it was a great strain. " One pair of hands to do everything," he had written when he went to Glasshampton; but these poor broken-down priests involved a greater strain as he ruefully allowed on " body, soul and purse." And yet . . .

It seems a work such as we can do, and I think it is of GOD, so I buckle on my armour. You see, there is no place

[1] This need was never supplied, and the unfinished south-west corner remains as it was, in temporary repair. It is used for the electric plant, wash-house, storage of garden tools, etc.

in C. of E. for such. In the Roman Church they go to the great Monasteries. If a priest takes a false step, we inhibit him, and he may go to the dogs. I went to my Bishop about it, and though he was nice, he seemed mostly anxious not to incur responsibility.

There it is. I have just had three. One, I hope, will soon be restored to the Mission Field. One is mentally incapacitated, and one is paralysed down the left side. . . .

Many years later he writes when distressed at having to refuse such work:

You know for years I have dealt with such cases, and I am only refusing them for reasons of health and want of help.

I have always wanted to *show* them how to do it, and even now I never know when GOD will open the way. A little more man-power and about £1000 dropping from Heaven would at once set it in motion, for I should adapt the last of the ruins for the purpose.

Then I should leave behind a well-defined Life of Prayer and a work of mercy beside it. It is terribly needed, and absolutely nothing is done officially.

Such a work did not disturb Father William's solitary life or prayer. It was like the open window with the curtain of the Anchoress' cell; it was a blessed means of touching the world he had left. Like St. Anthony of old, he had gone into the cave for prayer and solitude. Towards the end of his life he was ready to come out, or rather to receive within his cave, at the call of God, the outcast and the fallen, but from ministering to these he always returned to his solitary life and rule as a monk. It was this solitary life of prayer that increasingly brought home to him the great need of some refuge in the Church of England where priests who had fallen by the way could find recovery and renewal.

In spite of his intention to " close the doors " of his Monastery and live his own life of prayer, his generous hospitality could not refuse a guest or a case of need; to him, too, as to the inner vision of the Celt: " *Often, often, often comes the Christ in the stranger's guise* ", and such a Guest was never turned away from Glass-hampton. He writes in the last letter of this period:

Solemnity of St. Benedict, 1935.

There are three here in retreat and one just left. On

Saturday another priest from the slums of London and various callers—one a Russian lady, who writes.

A nice boy with a contemplative vocation who will wait a while to see if I can contrive to take him. And I am rather expecting the Abbot and the Father-Superior of the Order of the Holy Cross from America, and I think I told you of a Religious in Australia?

.   .   .   .   .   .

It might be that men will come from the ends of the earth to " found " something here? We cannot tell.

Keep this a secret with THE KING.

XIII

A SPIRITUAL GUIDE

Pour conduire son âme et celle des autres, le directeur n'a qu'une régle: Dieu; il va à Dieu, et il mène à Dieu.

RIBET.

BEFORE we speak of Father William as a priest and guide of souls, we must estimate at least in some degree his own attainment in spiritual things. That he had great gifts of discernment in dealing with souls and unbounded sympathy and compassion for the sinful and fallen is well known; but some of his earlier friends did not observe that his mind had been patiently trained to a firm intellectual grasp of the doctrines of the faith, and that he grew to be especially at home in moral theology, in the history and principles of the religious life and in the great central tradition of mystical theology.

The spring of Father William's own spiritual life lay in the particular emphasis he placed upon the doctrine of the Incarnation as being not only the taking of our nature into God but the entrance of God Himself, in the person of our Lord Jesus Christ, into the stuff of our humanity and everyday life, and therefore of the necessity of the evangelist also identifying himself with the people among whom he worked. He did not believe you could minister to poverty or sin from afar; you must enter it with your own life and share its environment and suffering. From this came the decision in his early life as a priest to live the same life and under the same conditions as the toiling poor around Vauxhall bridge, but though he could live in the common lodging-house, he could not rid himself of his security of position. The call to the three vows of poverty, chastity and obedience followed as a natural sequence, and through these he rid himself of the prerogative of social caste and property. When threatened with an action for libel if he persisted in unveiling the conditions of life and housing in a north-country town, he could say as he laid his hand on his habit, " You can do your worst; this is all I have and all you will get! "

To *see* a demand and to embrace what he saw in one and the

self-same moment was typical of Father William. He never lingered on the way. He had a deep fear of missing what God held out to him. So when he saw the need of the life of prayer behind the activities of the Church, her priests and Religious Orders, as the cause of much of their failure, he felt that need as a Call to himself. But this was a more serious matter than the first call to the Religious Life, for it seemed to deny the way he had already come. Was he not bound to the active work of S.D.C.? He had been Novice Master and was now Superior, sincerely and deeply attached to its rule and spirit, as well as to the Fathers and Brothers of the Society. So he set himself to test the Call, and wait and learn patience. The *interior* response could be made, but the external must wait. He must understand the meaning of God's Will in his own life. There must not only be the Call, but the *way* opened by God.

" The years of Vigil " changed the forceful impetuosity of the natural man into the tempered instrument of God's purpose. In a letter on pages 67–68 after his return from the eighteen months of waiting at Oxford he writes : " So you see I have had my conversion." And he asks for prayers. This, of course, was not the first conversion, which is the realization of sin and the need of God, and which leads to the mortification of all which is against God, the discipline of the flesh and the way of detachment and of the Cross. Father William passed through this stage in his early life and work, and is for us in later life a shining example of the simplicity which is found, not only by the negative way, but by the positive attachment to the Divine Will. He became *pliable*—a character to which the classical symbol of the wax and the seal could be used. This conversion, after long waiting, was the assurance that he was in the way of God's Will and was being moulded to the Divine Will by the happenings of the life around him, so he was content to wait on till God opened the way for him.

In all his later life we see this note of joy in following the Will of God and in the use of His creatures. The certainty that the responsibility was not his, but God's—" If men do not come, that is not my responsibility, but His ". He worked not for God, but *with* God, and this was the source of his supreme influence with souls, and of the abiding serenity and peace of his own life.

He underwent much arduous buffeting on the waves of the ocean of life. Few men knew better than he the meaning of the words, " Thou hast taken me up and cast me down ", but the inner peace was never disturbed. He was *in* the boat with the Master, but the Master was the Pilot and ruler of his life.

It must have been evident that under this life of serene peace and assurance of God's Will there was another life going on of discipline, austerity and penance. We saw this in his early life both as a priest and Religious. But it was not an austerity practised as an end in itself, but as a means to an end. His teaching was clear on this point. He said:

> At times in one's life austerity and penance has a use like a Doctor's prescription against any particular disease of sloth or any weakness in our nature's rebellion to the Divine Call.
>
> Used in this way it does not create hardness or self-pleasing in spiritual attainment. It creates a character in which a certain measure of austerity is always present and finds itself in the acceptance of GOD's Will which is just part of the wholeness of the surrender.

In the early days at Glasshampton there were quite a number of these; they were just the ordinary happenings of the life of poverty. If it was cold—well, it *was* cold, that was all, and you went on with your job just the same.

The Rev. Gilbert Shaw writes of the days before electric light and central heating were thought of in the monastery:

> I remember one Shrove Tuesday when I had gone down to see Father William preparatory to a Retreat, at a time when the Severn was frozen over at Worcester, sitting with him in the Library when the sole heat in the monastery was the one candle by which we were sitting and talking—each of us wrapped in our cloaks!

His vow of poverty was kept both in spirit and in letter. His cupboard might be bare, but he left it until God replenished it.

Sir Sydney Lea,[1] a close neighbour and friend of all the Glasshampton years, writes:

> I have never known anybody with such an atmosphere. You knew at once you were in the presence of a Saint. You received at once a tonic, which stimulated all the good in you, and a disinfectant which paralysed all one's badness. Temptations could not tempt, the desires and worries of

---

[1] Sir Sydney Lea of Dunley Hall, Stourport, one of the executors of Father William's Will, and trustee of the present buildings of the monastery.

this life faded. He brought you calm and joy and the Peace of GOD. No one could be unaware of this.

It was not what he said, and it was not what he did; it was what he was, and it was always the same.

It was this which brought men like Mr. Stanley Baldwin, at this time of which we are writing Prime Minister of England,[1] to be a frequent visitor to the monastery; to value the quiet interludes of an hour's talk with its solitary inmate, to sit in the garden or the Guest Parlour for a quiet talk, and drink in its peace—to find something missing if such a visit were not possible.

At a time of acute national crisis shortly after Father William's final departure for hospital, Mr. Baldwin wrote saying how tremendously he would miss a visit which he always looked forward to as a time of spiritual refreshment and quickening.

Father William used to tell him, " I have been a Bolshevist as long as I can remember ". So the friendship was not a political one.

Another friendship of these later years with far-reaching influence was with Arthur Smallwood, Director of Greenwich Hospital [2] and builder of the Naval School at Holbrook, with its magnificent Chapel for the orphan lads of Greenwich, removing them from the asphalt-paved playgrounds of crowded Greenwich, to the green fields and open waters of the estuary at Harwich known as " Holbrook ". Here lads are educated on the lines of a public school, with their own masters and chaplain, their hospital, playing-field and home farm.

Mr. Smallwood had not known Father William until at the suggestion of a friend he paid his first visit to Glasshampton in 1924. From that date he was a frequent visitor, finding in Father William's own life the understanding of his desire to bring the life of the Greenwich orphans as far as possible under

[1] Now Earl Baldwin of Bewdley, and owner of Astley Hall, overlooking the hill of Glasshampton.

[2] Arthur William Smallwood, C.B.E., also Executor of Fr. William's Will and Trustee of Glasshampton. 1897, Civil Service appointment to Admiralty; 1914–1918, Director of Shipping Contracts; 1921–1934, Director of Greenwich Hospital. Holbrook was completed and opened by the Prince of Wales in 1933. The money for this school was given by Mr. Reade of New Zealand, a legacy when it matured amounting to one million pounds. This sum, together with the estate known as Holbrook, was given by Mr. Reade as a thank-offering for the work of the Sailors of the Merchant Service during the War of 1914–1918. The school Chapel has a capacity for 1100. The Lady Chapel is built as a memorial to Mr. Reade. Arthur Smallwood died March 9, 1938, and is buried at Oxted in Surrey.

the influence of the Christian faith and the normal surroundings of home. At Greenwich they were, from the age of eight years, entirely in the care of naval men. At Holbrook the boys in their respective houses found home, masters and matron and nurses when needed. This discipline of a naval school and upbringing is still kept, combined with the atmosphere of a home.

Mr. Smallwood, as director of this great public charity for the orphans of merchant seamen, carried the spirit of Glasshampton into his work of education, and left it as his legacy to the school of his creation. After his retirement in 1934 he devoted himself to the care of Father William in the last years of his life.

Father William's reverence for the work of the Holy Spirit in the soul, together with a complete elimination of himself, made him an ideal director, not only of those called by God to some special vocation but of great sinners who had been brought to an equally great repentance. However deep such a soul might have fallen, the instinctive respect with which Father William met the penitent, both within and without the tribunal of penance, gave to him both hope and encouragement to persevere.

For the future life of his penitent he did not lay down many rules and prohibitions. He demanded some step which committed the penitent to the new orientation of his life and sent him out to fulfil it.

In a work of this kind it is not possible to give many extracts from letters of spiritual direction, but there are some too valuable to miss. Writing to a Religious about the formation of the religious life, he said:

> There were two things I used to see. One was the absolute need of interior silence and recollection, and the other the need of exterior bearing even when kneeling at prayer, and also orderliness and quiet deportment. Mother Frances Raphael is so good about all that, and says it is not fussiness, but equivalent to learning to finger if you are to become a professional pianist or violinist. I also saw the need of manual labour, silence, and reading, and even enclosure. I expect I was far in advance of my place and time. I see that now, and it must have led not a little to the perplexities of those years for myself and for others.

He wrote to one seeking vocation in the turmoil of the world:

> No, yours is not an " awful confession ". It reads as of a

Franciscan, and that outlook is in my blood too. For there are two ways: the recluse who can't bear looking at even the beautiful things from GOD for fear of not seeing the Giver, and St. Francis, who revelled in all Nature because it carried him into the Presence of GOD.

So the real art of being in the way of the Will of GOD is for each to follow the personal guidance of the Holy Spirit. Else it is like applying a plaster merely on the surface, instead of being as GOD has made you by seeing to it that all the ordering of your life springs out of your real self *from* GOD.

And to another:

It is good of you to give me your confidence, and I value it very much, though I am bad at expressing what I feel. It wins my poor love, and I can assure you that I will keep your name and your work at my Mass every morning, and try to help you to keep in the stream of GOD's love and grace.

You must leave all the past in His hands for healing and for fructifying. We must concentrate on the Cult of the passing moment. That, I find, is a golden secret. He saves our past from our failure—fills up where it has been imperfect. He is our SUCCESS.

I am so grieved about your little girl, and will give her my poor prayers.

How can *I* guide you? You have been very faithful in the many difficult sacrifices you have been called upon to make. I believe there are some people GOD chooses to make sacrifices for Him. He puts into their hands great treasures—they are good and holy and true, and there would be no sin if they embraced them, but, because they love GOD more than His gifts, they give them back to Him.

I fancy that is the great secret of saintliness, and it lies at the very root of the Christian Life. And in the case of marriage the ideal is not the seeking of the satisfaction of ourselves, but it is the gift of self which *is* sacrifice at the highest, which is true love.

And again:

I am sure you are right to accommodate yourself to your family surroundings. A good text would be: " Show me your charity to others, and I will tell you your love for GOD ". And both courtesy and gratitude make great demands which may not rightly be ignored.

The relaxation is not what you have sought. It is strangely

imposed upon you, and I am sure if you use it with thanksgiving—even to the full—you will derive great blessings for the future. . . . I am speaking out of my own experience when I was swept to the Riviera.

To a Nurse:

Perhaps that *Crossness* is apt to creep into most lives as the years count up. Well, not so much " creep in " as assail. Probably at root it is self-will and pride being aroused. Try to face it out with yourself in prayer, and ask for grace to be submissive. Like all the trials and temptations that come to us, it is not meant to set us back in the spiritual life, but to give us the opportunity to grow and make progress —to lift us up.

If we can accept the happenings as they come in the spirit of loving submission (realizing GOD permits them to come and that therefore they *must* be for our good), we shall avoid the thing that really hurts us—viz., our rebellion and resistance— and we shall find that the acceptance of our humiliation has done us much good. " Crossness " generally springs out of annoyances at our own limitations or the perversity of persons and things. You should form a resolution in your daily prayer about it, and be careful! for what the Devil wants is not so much that we shall be cross, but that we shall be cross *because* we have been cross!

On suffering. To a Religious:

I was grateful to you for writing at that length, though you are still, I fear, in pain. I am very sorry. Your request was for a Mass that you might recover quickly *if it is GOD'S Will*. It came to me in a very vivid way that there is really only *one* prayer—viz., that we and all GOD's creatures may do His Will in all things. The agony of prayer is giving up ourselves and our own wills, and accepting blindly all that seems to go so much against our prospects. Even when we grow into the knowledge and love of GOD there would seem to remain at all times this wrestling against self. So it was the same end whichever way one offered the prayer, if it was true prayer. And I knew what your request for the Mass meant for you. It is wonderful how GOD sends us all only what is best. It is, I am sure, out of the bitterest and most painful experiences that the truest and most enduring blessings can grow. When you speak of reading St. John of the Cross and reordering your life, I learn a great lesson for myself. I know I ought not to wish it were otherwise than it is for you, but that you are lifted up in the acceptance and use of what GOD sends. With all my heart I try now to do that. . . .

Whitsun Monday.

All I can prescribe out of my own experience is to abide patiently till the soul relaxes—it is strung up. It needs to be let free from all thought and strain, and simply to bathe itself in the ocean of GOD's love. Do nothing itself— but let GOD do all. Utter surrender. Then it becomes still, tranquil, and goes out to GOD and rests. This is a feeble expression of what can't be expressed.

Michaelmas 1933.

This letter was written to a third person in reference to one who in intense spiritual suffering had sought refuge at Glasshampton:

Thank you for your letter. It did not seem opportune to give the letter to D. S. We talked together. On the whole I think there is perhaps improvement, but still that heavy suffering. The happy thing is we grow into a fuller experience of how to use this inestimable gift of GOD which most of us started by having no use for at all. The contemplation of Our Blessed Lord and His Holy Mother indeed teaches us and leads us *into* the inexhaustible mystery of suffering which is ever mingled with sacrifice and love, and is bound up with the sharing in sympathy of the Cross with others.

To someone troubled with controversy about Rome:

Apart from all controversy, I find myself by the providence of GOD in the Church of England. It has always been to me a very difficult and trying position, and there has been the temptation to escape those trials and difficulties by changing my " obedience ".

If the Church of England could be proved to be no Church at all—*i.e.*, not a part of the Church Catholic—I should be bound to come out of it. But the Church of England cannot be proved to be no Church at all, so to change in my case would be to escape something I did not like to bear. I know in my heart of hearts that all the baptized are in the Mystical Body of CHRIST. I should not go out of the Church if I submitted to Rome, but I should go out of the particular set of difficult circumstances in which I believe GOD has placed me.

The experts on either side can make their case to appear conclusive, but they can't convince you that the flow of the supernatural does not reach you through the Sacraments of the English Church.

This is a hurried and, I fear, very imperfect statement, but you will know the spirit in which it is written.

I shall bear you in mind, and I shall surely know your decision will be for the highest you can see.

GOD bless and guide you always.

Did you ever read Baron von Hügel's *Letters*? I think he best expresses what I feel and believe.

Easter Monday. To C. F.

Of course I ought to have presented you with " Blossoming ", because you helped me so much over it. I am glad you think it serviceable. It has been extraordinarily well received. Even the R.C.s say it is *the* best short account of the Monastic ideal. So I have to beware of pride and vainglory!

I suppose the world will always be in a tangle. I think the Church would be so much more powerful if it were disentangled from the world and from possessions *everywhere*. It is almost impossible for the ordinary man to see anywhere now the loveliness of what can be seen in the N.T. Not at Canterbury nor at Rome. If we look at the Perfect Example, His Glory is His utter poverty and disregard of worldliness as such. But there . . .

On Monasticism. 25 *March.*

The main fault of the article is that it is soul-less and that there is no mention of GOD or of the Saviour. It speaks of monasticism as a human institution springing up from below. But its power and fruitfulness is derived from its source—*i.e.*, GOD.

Monasticism is no more a failure than Christianity itself. Neither can be wiped out as impossible or useless. Individuals fail to be true to them. The ideal of both is the same, and such ideals can never be fully realized or sustained here upon earth. It is sufficient if we strive faithfully. We reach the goal hereafter.

1 *May.*

The writer, all the way through, calmly separates Monasticism from the Church. It can't be done, even historically. Monasticism is a vital part of the Church. Thousands upon thousands of Bishops, Archbishops, Cardinals and Popes have been used by the Church, by transferring them from their Monasteries to activity as high officials.

Besides, in the mind of GOD there is no such thing as division—to Him the whole Mystical Body is one and entire. It is the deranged mind of man that invents division.

Monasticism is the Church herself acting through some of her members, who are ever striving to get back to the purity of the Divine ideal, the ideal not discoverable by man, but revealed to him by GOD.

Quite rightly and very humbly in monasticism, the monks begin by cleansing the inner courts of the Sanctuary of their own souls (there is absolutely nothing in monasticism to even suggest " flying buttresses " !). The only hope for GOD's Church is for the individual members, one by one, to aim at the ideal GOD has revealed—that is the highest contribution anyone can make, and no one can be of much use in larger schemes, until he has achieved that. It is utterly inaccurate to say " that in doing so the monk has manufactured an ideal of his own outside the Church ".

To a Solitary who was kept awake by ducks.

St. Mary of the Snows, 1931.

Yes! even saints and ducks can be used to batter! But it makes us more determined to be with GOD. The cattle congregate beneath my window, and the owls assemble on the big oak a few yards away, so I am surrounded by the sounds I love to hear, but they tend to assist in keeping me awake when I feel I ought to be asleep. Yet all the time I know I am in a world where nothing can go wrong.

I am slowly learning, that I must make the proper use of *all* that happens unsolicited. I used to think I had to cast aside, as useless for GOD's purposes, the things I had not reckoned for—they were hindrances. Now, I begin to see they come to bring me the choicest of blessings.

XIV

PERSONALITY AND CHARACTER

Character is the power to keep the selected motive dominant in life.
MÜNSTERBERG.

HERE was a personality richly endowed, wonderfully deepened by experience, and strikingly unified by grace. At this point a backward glance towards origins, much briefer though more comprehensive than our first, will enable us to find the roots of several characteristic strains in this vivid and many-sided nature.

First and most notable his religious intensity. The Sirrs were descended from Lot Sers, a Huguenot pastor who claimed descent from the de Sers of Montrédon in the South of France. This Huguenot pastor came to London as a refugee, and his son Francis Sirr of St. Clement Dane's, Westminster, seems to have become a well-to-do West India silk merchant. From this French strain Father William undoubtedly inherited his deeply religious character, his great vivacity and resilience, his unfailing courtesy and something of his power of influencing others.

There was also a military strain. The family in a later generation having moved to Ireland, three of the Sirrs were great figures in their country in the promotion of civil order and the suppression of rebellion. Joseph Sirr, after distinguished service in the Army, became High Sheriff of the County of Dublin. Following in his footsteps, Father William's great-grandfather and grandfather both held commissions in the regular army, and later did notable service for the Crown in the difficult and responsible post of Town-Major, a post which also carried with it, as had Joseph's office, a residence in Dublin Castle. His father, who was born there, though himself a civil servant by profession, was devoted in his service as a volunteer—he held commissions in the Royal Westminster Militia and the Honourable Artillery Company. It is not surprising that with such an ancestry Father William was notably military both in disposition and in carriage. His soldierly instincts gave him a special admiration for such Christian heroes as St. Ignatius Loyola and Vicomte de Foucauld.

Irish blood came into the Sirr family only through the marriage of William's grandfather, Henry Sirr, to Elizabeth, daughter of James d'Arcy of Hyde Park, Co. Westmeath. From this Irish grandmother Father William inherited those undoubted Irish traits which led to his being spoken of as an Irishman: his great generosity to friend or foe, his impulsiveness, which sometimes led him into errors of judgment in trusting fallen human nature, and his inability to turn a deaf ear to any tale of suffering.

He was Irish also in his great talent for reading aloud, in his power to entertain and amuse others, and his gift of humour, in which these capacities were grounded. Indeed, none can read his letters without being struck by this gift, or observing how often it saved him in situations of disaster which in others might have led to despair. He had a hot temper, but how few of those who have attained to any measure of sanctity have not! How many parallels could be found in the lives of the Saints for such an incident as the memorable lapse we have recorded in the period of his preparation for ordination.

He always regarded the tongue as an unruly member, and there was something in the grave gentleness and recollection of his natural manner of speaking which instinctively recalled the presence of God to those with whom he was. He had not a little to try him by reason of the ailments, physical and spiritual, of his very varied household, as well as, in later years, his own bad health. But his serenity remained unimpaired. For many years he had living with him an old lay-brother of another Community which had died out. For all his goodwill, Brother F.'s infirmities caused many very difficult situations. "He was wonderfully patient with this brother," writes one who was often at Glasshampton during those years, ". . . indeed, I can only remember one occasion on which he rebuked him. Brother F. had completely wrecked the arrangements Father William had made to give tea in his garden to some villagers. I happened to bring something into the kitchen, and I heard him say, ' Brother, you won't do that again, will you? ' "

One who was allowed to spend his preparation for Holy Orders at Glasshampton writes of the corporate recreations for guests at that time:

> Recreations at Glasshampton were quite unique in their way, and might not have been so successful and happy under the direction of a Superior less controlled and disciplined than

Father William habitually was. He would often spend an hour with his guests between supper and Compline. He would tell story after story recounting some humorous incidents with vivid pantomime and laughter. He always had himself, his listeners, and the story of the moment, under complete control. When the bell rang for Compline there was a sudden silence as he withdrew into himself and his habitual grave recollection.

Another recalls his first delighted realisation after such an hour that conversation, however entertaining, had been directed (whether consciously or unconsciously) in such a way as to keep the prayerful mind of our host—and in a lesser fashion those of his guests—intent throughout upon people and matters that required the spiritual succour of informal as well as formal intercession. The realisation came to him first on an Ember day.

" Hush! ", Father William had said suddenly, " do you hear anything? "

" No," we replied.

" *I do.* I can hear the ordinands in every Palace in the country —they ought to be praying, but they are really busy *swearing*! "

We remembered that trying and expensive proceeding of oath-taking which in most dioceses so tiresomely disturbs the ordination retreat. And so we went on to recall other more poignant experiences and opportunities of the ordination retreat and of the beginnings of the ministry.

As we see, Father William could and did pray in any conditions, but he could not conceive of the life of prayer except as lived in the atmosphere of a disciplined order. Disorder and dirt were abhorrent to him, as well as any want of simplicity.

Whether as a young missioner, in the architect's office or in the wine-merchant's warehouse, Father William showed great capacity for business, and in his years as Superior of S.D.C. there was the same far-seeing capacity for creating and building up new developments in the Community. At Glasshampton to create, as he did, a monastery out of a ruin, needed not only business power, but the artistic and architectural gifts which had been trained in the offices of Street & Cockerell and Professor Aitchison. In Glasshampton we see no trace of the Arab Hall of Leighton House, but we do see the chaste beauty of Mr. Street's work.

He was essentially creative. Wherever he was and in all he

undertook there was development and growth. Order appeared as if by magic out of disorder, quietness and peace out of strife and conflict. He had a quick critical judgment but these traits he brought under discipline. There are few, if any, who ever heard him say a bitter or unkind thing. He could repeat the story of an experience or an interview with an unfriendly person, or one who had hurt him deeply and give its truthful setting, but he did not pass judgment on the author of the incident as necessarily wanting in charity to himself. If he was opposed in any vital matter and he was sure he was right, his reaction was sure and to the point. He saw what to do and carried it through. An instance of this occurred during the building of Glasshampton. When the buildings were partly finished and the Chapel and its altar ready for hallowing, Father William, with his idea of authority in the Church, naturally desired episcopal sanction for the work he had done. Bishop Yeatman-Biggs, who had welcomed him to the Diocese to live the life of a Contemplative Religious, had left Worcester, and was now Bishop of Coventry. Father William wrote to his then Diocesan, the Bishop of Worcester, asking him if he would bless the new building and hallow the altar. But Bishop Pearce felt it his duty to decline to visit Glasshampton, nor would he allow Bishop Chandler, Father William's friend of Poplar and South African days, to do so. In his distress Father William wrote to Bishop Yeatman-Biggs requesting the favour of an interview, which was accorded him at Lambeth Palace. No stranger cargo was ever discharged from a taxi at these doors than Father William carrying with him, wrapped in a blanket, the altar-stones of Glasshampton. He had brought them to be hallowed by the Bishop in Lambeth Chapel. So did Lambeth and Glasshampton meet, and God's blessing was bestowed at the heart of the Church of England on the altars of the monastery and the work of its founder.

With practical gifts also Father William was richly endowed. He could carpenter, garden and cook, and even make his own bread; much of this he taught himself at Glasshampton. His attitude to the necessities of life was refreshingly simple. With the aid of steamers and such contrivances he just put the food on and abandoned it in hope, while he went on with his offices and regular life, and it generally was all right. He had difficulty in teaching others to cook with the primitive appliances he allowed to himself. The aspirant in the kitchen did not usually find within himself the ability to weigh and measure time and substance which worked such magic in Father William's own efforts as a cook. As the years went on and he lived a solitary life, it is doubtful whether he "cooked" at all, and whether he did not find, as the Curé d'Ars had done, all he needed in bread-and-cheese, salad and potatoes and other foods nearest to poverty and the soil.

He could draw and design and paint. The only example of the last is a pleasing water-colour sketch painted, it would seem, in Highgate cemetery near his parents' grave. It was sent to his friend, Mr. John Sutton, and had clearly been at once recreation and prayer.

He had a great love of animals and an amazing influence over them. At one time at Glasshampton he had a dog, Betsey—she lived in the kitchen and garden, and was never allowed in any other part of the monastery. He had trained her in silence, and she was never heard to bark in the monastery. Her devotion to her master was unmistakable.

At other times there were Stella and Flossie, and later a beautiful Persian tortoiseshell cat which in her old age, because of the multitude of her offspring, was called "Granny". They lived outside in the garden, and followed Father William about in his work.

To the end of his life Father William retained his Franciscan love of all God's creatures, his interest in farming and farm cattle, in birds and flying insects. He noticed their coming and going—nothing was too small or insignificant—and he invariably spoke of them as God's creatures.

There is a delightful letter written at a time when, in the depths of winter, he was exercising himself in early rising and night-watching. He found his vigils had companions—a moth and a fly.

> The moth lives in Chapel, but sleeps a good deal! The fly walks on the window, but only when the sun shines. Just now he is asleep in the corner. I am greatly interested in them and am always tempted to add to the Benedicite " O ye fly and moth, bless ye the Lord " . . .

To those who visited Glasshampton, the dignity, radiance and awestruck reverence of Father William's demeanour at prayer in chapel are unforgettable. One who used to visit him as a boy from ten years old onwards until his years as an undergraduate at Oxford, has a specially vivid memory of this.

> The way in which he said the Mass and Offices—especially the slow, meditative reading of the Psalms—and the wonderful way he said " O God " and " O Lord ", each time joyfully greeting the one boundlessly rich Reality in Whom his soul rested, gave one a little insight into the life of contemplative prayer which lay beneath all that he said and did.   In the time for silent prayer I can still see him in the corner of the chapel, using no kind of book or notes, absolutely still, the evening sun streaming in through the little window over the door on to the gold-and-white Tabernacle veil, the window of the Cherubim veiling their faces above, a stillness complete except for the distant humming of the bees.

Beneath the surface of this attractive and gifted personality there lay a will of iron—softened and sheathed in depths of compassion and of understanding sympathy for the weak and sinful. He would speak of himself with a twinkle in his eye as " I am a very obstinate man ". He did not add that the " obstinate man " who had sought God in his youth, and triumphed over the difficulties of his boyhood and young manhood going out to seek the " down and out " and to " compel them to come in ", had been transmuted by the long discipline of the years of vigil into waiting *upon the Will of God*, and transmuted yet again in the still longer years of apparent failure into an instrument not *alongside* the Will of God, to use his own words, but welded within it so that he moved unswervingly in ever closer union *with* that Will. In the bitterest experience of disappointment or failure he found here not only his peace, but the rod of direction for himself as to his next step in the way before him.

His understanding of the word " failure " came to mean for him not that with which we endow it, but a word of union with our Lord. It has often appeared in this story of his life—it was the last word on his lips as he left his beloved monastery for the last time, knowing he would not see it again.

At this point illness of a kind hitherto unknown to him had come upon him. It had culminated in severe abdominal pains which suggested an immediate operation. His devoted spiritual son, Arthur Smallwood, who had been with him during these last months, was waiting upon him; the car to take him away was at the door.

The Rev. Sidney King writes of this moment:

> I called quite unexpectedly, not knowing he was ill, and was told of his serious condition and that it was not possible to see him. I asked that he might know that I, an old friend, was at the Monastery unexpectedly, and if he liked to see me I would be glad; but, if not, all was well. He said he would be pleased to see me, but the time was short. I found him on his bed, waiting to be taken away for his final leaving, as indeed it was.
>
> Here let me say that as the years went on and I saw the Monastery take its form—the cells for Monks all prepared and yet no Monks—I ceased to enquire if any fresh Postulants had come, feeling it must be painful to him to speak of it.
>
> On this last morning when I saw him on his bed his face lit up in welcome. I asked if I might pray with him, and I knelt at what was his last prayer in the Monastery. I commended him to God and besought God's peace upon him.
>
> When I rose from my knees he said, looking me straight in the face, serene and untroubled, apropos of nothing said in the interview or in the prayers, "*We must not mind being a failure—Our Lord died on the Cross a failure*". Words I can never forget, nor the tone of his serene, quiet repose in the Will of God. I knew that in that absolute surrender of his will to God, he had entered into the victorious mind of our Saviour on the Cross and knew the ineffable peace which only the Saints very near to God can know; and into which nothing can break nor destroy.

The whole of Father William's life and devotion seems summed up in this his farewell to years of labour and hope and prayer at Glasshampton.

His tired body was to return to rest in the little quadrangle near the great Crucifix, his soul having passed into the keeping of our Lord Who alone sees and understands the true meaning of success or failure.

XV

THE LAST YEARS

. . . 'tis the essence of this blessed being to hold ourselves within the divine will, whereby our own wills are themselves made one.

.   .   .   .

and his will is our peace; it is that sea to which all moves that it createth and that nature maketh.

DANTE, *Paradiso*, Canto III.

THE illness from which Father William suffered when he left Glasshampton for the last time was not found to need an immediate operation, but there was a weak heart and high blood pressure, and he was told he must not again return to his monastery and live alone.

At this moment the owner of the Astley estate, the Rev. Cecil Jones, Chaplain to the Community of the Holy Name at Malvern, was also seriously ill, and the Reverend Mother asked Father William if he could give Mr. Jones such help in his work as he was able to do. For some time he lived in lodgings at Malvern close to the convent.

His anxiety as to the future of his beloved monastery was considerably increased at seeing in the public press the preliminary notice of the sale of the whole of the Astley estate, including the monastery and the surrounding farms, either together or in lots. With increased death-duties and family claims, Father William saw that Mr. Jones had no alternative but to sell, and also that he could not take out of the sale the small centre portion of Glasshampton monastery standing as it did in the very heart of the estate, and depending for its approach upon the right-of-way through the Park and surrounding fields. But this did not lessen his anxiety for the future.

Father William did not live to see the sale, nor to know that at a later date the property, having passed through the hands of a new owner, would be purchased by his executors through the help of friends as a memorial to himself. It seemed as though God would not resolve the faith and trust of His faithful priest by allowing him to know how soon by the help of friends the monastery was to be secured.[1]

Though in failing health in these last years, Father William kept up his vivid interest in the life of the Church and her work. He had always profoundly distrusted anything like publicity or what he would call " stunts "; and he shrank from such things as High Mass at the Stadium, which at that time was occupying the energies of many of the younger men—things good, perhaps, in themselves, but he felt they distracted men from self-dedication and the evangelizing work which was the great need of the Church.

A letter written in February 1935 expresses his mind very clearly:

> Looking into the future of the Church in its work man-wards, I see no hope in the present methods. The Church of England has miserably failed GOD. She for centuries had the immense advantages of wealth, buildings and State support, and look at the teeming masses she never touches. I would not knock it down, but I would bring up a new way, and what is there but the apostolic way of deep consecration? This way cannot be sustained, so the ages of the Church show, without some form of the Religious Life. I want to gather up all the enthusiasm of the " groups " into some such method of continuity. Even so, because of the infirmity of human nature, it tends to cool down and to degenerate. But it is the only way that has proved most secure down the centuries. One reason is that it frees the individual of all the responsibilities, cares and anxieties of the ordinary clergyman. And it is this entanglement that has weighed down, and is weighing down, and dividing the attention of the Church at large today. Beyond this, it is only the consecrated *life* that has the power of penetrating the depths of the souls of others. All the passionate oratory and all the endless organisations only choke and leave no passage for the Word of GOD to have free course. It is this apostolic *life* that thrills the soul as we read the Gospels, Acts and Epistles. And such a life needs a garden set apart by our Lord for the cultivation of His choicest flowers. Whether it is the Franciscan, the Mirfield or the Glasshampton way will be shewn for each individual.
>
> What we are both concerned about is the best method of

[1] In 1936 Glasshampton Park and the monastery and some 800 acres of land were bought in one lot by Mr. Alex Comley. The advowson of the parish of Astley was not included in the sale, and was vested by Mr. Jones in the Guild of All Souls. But the future of the monastery was wholly obscure at the time of Father William's death.

sustaining a continuity of self-consecration for the Evangelist. I think the best thing is to be at the beck and call of GOD. Even St. Clare or St. Anthony must be prepared to leave their beloved Cell if He wills. Absolute consecration leaves freedom for this.

. . . . . .

. . . We *must* try to fit in our personal vocation with the movement of GOD in our age. Perhaps I departed from this by going to Glasshampton, though I went under direction and obedience. And the end of that is yet to be seen. . . .

I feel sure the enclosed monk for the life of prayer must come sooner or later, and GOD will raise up the Founder and the vocations. I sometimes think these are nearer than we imagine. . . .

. . . . . .

At the end of Lent in this last year of his life he was asked by Canon Shirley, Headmaster of King's School, Canterbury, to give an address the evening before the Confirmation to the boys who were to be confirmed the following day in the Cathedral, and to hear confessions. He felt this was indeed God's call to him to leave his cell. He sought the faithful intercessions of his friends and spiritual children Anchoresses and Religious—the power-house, as he would say, of the Church—and made his own preparation.

He writes to a friend:

I want to thank you for the help of prayer for me and the boys at King's School, Canterbury. I found a printed paper for me with just on ninety names of those to be confirmed. I spoke to them in the Crypt. Afterwards they kept me busy hearing their confessions till 10 p.m. I had not asked them to come but when, after the address, I went to the Chapel I found the boys lined up in a queue waiting for me. I started again after Mass and breakfast, and only got through by 12. the time of the Confirmation. I took the last boy up after the Confirmation had begun. I think most of them made their Confession. The Archbishop said the Mass in the Crypt on Sunday morning to give them their first Communion. The whole School present. Four of us administered, and we communicated over 200 boys.

Will you say a thanksgiving for them and for me, and pray for their perseverance? Nothing quite like that has often happened there—certainly not since the Reformation.

After his return to Malvern it was evident he could not do even the partial work of the Chaplaincy, and he was again seriously ill with heart failure. Mr. Smallwood, who gave him the devotion of a son, stayed with him during this time. With rest there was a rallying of his powers, but some decision had to be made as to his future. Another devoted spiritual son wrote offering to come and be with him at Glasshampton to care for him to the end, but Father William would not permit this act of generosity.

He wrote to one of his spiritual children:

> Happenings thick and fast within and without have brought me and all that concerns me into a fluid condition. I dare not attempt to do anything, for GOD's never-failing providence *is* ordering all things. I have collapsed here, and do not know where GOD wants me to go next.
>
> I believe the only thing generally for us to do when things are so disturbed and difficult is to *transcend* them in penitence and prayer and go straight on through them. I have learned that, I think, from watching our LORD Himself. They comprise the toils of the pilgrimage, and without them we should be deprived of any resemblance to Him. . . . You will perceive how long it has taken me to write this and the mistakes I have made. I am coming to the end, but your prayers will sustain me.
>
> My grateful love,
Yours ever WILLIAM.
>
> I am hoping GOD will care for and preserve Glasshampton and fill it with monks, but I must not attempt to arrange anything, but leave it with GOD.

In the following October he was removed to the Homes of St. Barnabas at Dormans Park, Surrey, a home for invalid and aged priests. He was received with great courtesy and kindness, and rooms on the ground floor were placed at his disposal. There was a peculiar fitness that he who had so often found at St. Barnabas help and kindness for others in need should himself find here a place of refuge. It was accepted for himself as God's Will, and its inner significance was not missed. It was the last stooping down to share the lives of those broken by life's buffetings, and he made with them his last home.

He writes to a friend:

October 27, 1936.   *Homes of St. Barnabas,*
                                       Dormans, Surrey.

> I am much touched by your affectionate letter. I did not *search* for this place. It was all done for me. I could not

suggest going to Stanford to be a heavy burden. I am really quite helpless, and I am told shall require nursing from time to time.

I have capable people kindly watching Glasshampton to keep it for GOD if possible. Very difficult and expensive.

I do hope you are well. Forgive such a brief letter, I can't write much.

My love, GOD bless you,
Yours gratefully,
WILLIAM.

7.11.36.   *Dormans.*

I get many calls from the brethren. I give myself to them and go on with Office and prayer in between. Like you, it seems to be GOD's way with us. It preserves us from self-centredness, and is the way He uses those surrendered to Him. We may be quite happy about it. They come, these calls, we don't seek them. See it in Our Lord's life in the Gospels.

SS. Fabian & Sebastian (Jan. 20, 1937).

Homes of St. Barnabas,
Dormans, Surrey.

How badly I treat you! I have been pondering over what you say in your last letter. I suppose we are all subject to that experience from time to time, though not so much as we get older. You would miss the fellowship you have been accustomed to—not so much *fellowship* as intimate *friendship*. I suppose GOD moves us into new ways of life. He has done so with me, particularly in bringing me here and lifting the weight of Glasshampton. I experience many blessings in this place, but the greatest blessing of all is *loneliness*. I have more time alone than ever before, so that I have the opportunity of spending more time on Offices and prayer.

It does not follow that I pray better—in fact, I find it gets harder to be recollected and concentrate on GOD. But I am happy in that I have the great privilege in trying to offer more to Him. Of course GOD has so constituted us that we mostly need companionship, but He, alas, often strips us of these consolations as life goes on and gradually detaches much from us that we may become more attached to Him. We are very liable to pull things to ourselves. If we do that those very thoughts bring us trouble. The secret is to be wholly abandoned to GOD and let Him order our lives. Like Job, we then become able to say " The Lord gave and the Lord hath taken away, blessed be the name of the Lord ".

To Him there was no such thing as misfortune or accident.

I hope I have not tired you out with platitudes. When we

meet we can speak of these things.   Certainly I have come to
see my life in greater simplicity, and GOD has given me
the gift to be happy and peaceful whatever should happen,
and I leave myself and Glasshampton confidently in that
atmosphere.

Forgive me for daring to say so much.

My best love.

Yours gratefully,

WILLIAM.

At the end of February Father William had a fall. The
doctor thought the fall had been caused by a stroke. In the same
week he had another stroke, followed by several fits from clots
of blood on the brain. Mr. Smallwood had seen him a few days
previously, and spoke of the indescribable peace of the whole
atmosphere of the room in which he found Father William.
After the stroke Mr. Smallwood was sent for, and did not leave him
again until there had been a partial recovery.

> He slept most of the time, occasionally opening his eyes
> with the old penetrating look without recognising anyone.
> To the astonishment of Doctor and Nurse, after Holy Unction,
> he rallied into his composed and cheerful and humorous self,
> and lingered on for some weeks. He made his confession on
> Easter Eve, and rose at 4 a.m. on Easter Sunday morning
> (March 28th,) to prepare for his Easter Communion, and
> thus prepared passed away suddenly and quietly to that
> heavenly Communion which surely our Lord willed to give
> him with His own Hand.

A little company of his faithful friends gathered round the
grave in which he was laid to rest in Lingfield churchyard on
Easter Thursday. There could be no question of burial at
Glasshampton, for the property was passing into the hands of
strangers.

Friends from the old life of Plaistow and S.D.C. mingled with
friends of Glasshampton and representatives of Religious Communities. A working man stood silently with a bowl of earth,
which he sprinkled on the coffin at the prayer of committal [1]—
it was the old gardener of Glasshampton and the earth was from
the garden of the monastery.

From the moving tribute which Father Andrew of the S.D.C.
wrote at the time of his death, we take the following:

[1] The funeral was taken by the Warden of Saint Barnabas' Homes, the
Rev. Canon George.

Father William lived and died a member of S.D.C., for he had never been formally released. A little great man who had a very profound influence on the spiritual life of a large number of people. By permission of the Society he was set free to found an Order of enclosed Religious if he could. He brought into being the Monastery of " St. Mary at the Cross ", at Glasshampton, Shrawley, Worcestershire; but he was never able to found an Order. His monastery is a place of pilgrimage to which has come all manner of souls, who will rise up and call him blessed. He was extra-ordinary confessor to more than one enclosed Community and the spiritual director of more than one anchoress.

He was a man of great courage, and possessed the irresistible Irish charm and the spontaneous Irish devotion, though there was no brogue to garnish his speech.

The present Prime Minister loved to visit him, and Mr. Stanley Baldwin is only one of a host who would pay homage to his sincerity. He was a man of great prayer, and the deep peace of his soul shone out in the sunshine of his smile and in every gesture. Everyone who knew him loved him, and all who loved him will miss him; but those who will miss him most are souls who, deeply troubled, sought his aid, and souls who were seeking to walk in the higher paths of the mountains of righteousness who sought his counsel.[1]

So he has passed. The Angels and Saints must have given him a great welcome. To think of Father William is to bring Fra Angelico's picture of " the Saints in Paradise " to life again. Is it an idle fancy to think of his asking leave of that Blessed Company to go and search in the fields of Paradise, where there are many Mansions of the Redeemed for his " down and outs " and " thinking men "? How gladly would they welcome him! Could even Paradise itself be complete without this companionship, to one who, like his Master, has been spoken of as " the friend of sinners ".

.   .   .   .   .   .

[1] From *Church Times* of April 2, 1937.

XVI

THE RETURN HOME

In my end is my beginning.

On an evening in the summer of 1939 [1] just before sunset a little group of those who had known and loved Glasshampton stood waiting to receive again the body of its founder. Through the kind offices of Lord Baldwin, and by permission of the Home Secretary, the necessary authority had been received to re-inter the body of Father William in the garth of the monastery. It rests there today under the shadow of the north side of the monastery, in the sure and certain hope of a joyful resurrection where and when all things will be known and understood, and each one shall receive the due reward of his labour.

Father William of Glasshampton had run in the sign of the Holy Trinity a course marked by the commemoration of two great fathers of the Cistercian life. His birth into this world had taken place on January 24, the day on which St. Alberic died; his heavenly birthday was on March 28, the day of the death of his patron, St. Stephen Harding. When Alberic's body had been laid to rest,[2] Stephen gave utterance to the comfort that is ours. "He is gone from us, but not from God; and if not from God, then not from us, for this is the right and property of saints; that when they quit this life they leave their body to their friends and carry away their friends with them in their mind . . . Blessed is the lot—more blessed he to whom that lot has fallen—most blessed we to be carried up to such a Presence."

[1] It was on September 15, the octave of the feast of the Nativity of the Blessed Virgin, and itself the feast of the Seven Sorrows. The day had been for many years observed as the patronal festival of the Monastery of St. Mary at the Cross.

[2] St. Alberic is commemorated on January 26, the day of his burial. The day given for his death may be conjecture. St. Stephen Harding is generally commemorated on April 17th, March 28th being given to the great Franciscan St. John Capistran.

Spring, 1933.

" *Now there stood by the Cross of Jesus His Mother* "

To our Friends

FROM

The Companions of
Blessed Mary at the Cross.

Greetings to you all.

Not least among many marvellous recoveries the Anglican
Communion has made in the last hundred years is the vigorous
restoration of the Religious Life which had been so rudely
suppressed at the Reformation. We realise not only what has
already been done in this direction, but also how much more must
yet be achieved ere we reach the goal set before us. But whether
we consider the immediate past or the unknown future, we thank-
fully take courage and press on again.

Now as we look around at this stage of the revival we find
contemplative communities of women happily established in our
midst. This is the highest peak we have attained in the recovery
of the Religious Life. It gives promise that the men will soon
follow.

We cannot, however, forget the great shock it gave Newman,
those many years ago, when he first realised there were no monks
and nuns in the Church of England, and we wonder whether we
are sufficiently concerned to-day to find we are still left without
one established community of men set apart wholly for this
supreme work of prayer and mortification. Are we fully alive to
the serious loss it must be for the Church to remain bereft of monks
of this description?

There can be no doubt of the increasing need there is of men
who will make daring adventure in the field of prayer. We
mean men after the pattern of what Jacob once proved himself to
be. He determined he would by prayer win a blessing from God.
For this purpose he carefully sought and diligently planned to be
alone, and alone he wrestled in prayer through the long watches

of the night until the breaking of the day. "I will not let thee go unless thou bless me." He declared he had seen God face to face, and as a prince, he won power with God and with men. It is true he ever afterwards bore the marks of the struggle he had gone through—but he prevailed.

It is men like that the Church needs so desperately today— men who will deliberately go apart to be with God alone, and stay there. They must be men wholly surrendered, and determined with dauntless courage to follow God through every tedious and painful vicissitude, and to endure in prayer right on to the very end, whatever the cost may be. That is the way prescribed by God, and it is in that direction such men of God have always gone. "I give myself unto prayer."

"The help that is done upon earth, God doeth it himself." But He deigns to ask for our co-operation as fellow-workers together with Him. God will not consent to act in loneliness.

Think—a divided Christendom has to be reunited, a distracted world has to be mended, all nations have to be brought to do Him service. These are blessings we all yearn for. And these are blessings we know God wills to give. Indeed, He is even now holding them out and waiting to bestow them upon us. Yet not without our utmost co-operation. Wherein, then, do we fail?

It is not in activities that we are in danger of falling short. In some respects our activities are excessive. It is in prayer and mortification we sorely need strengthening. And it is to monks we must look to help us to fill up this deficiency.

In our recovery of the Religious Life we have reversed the true order in which the Religious Life originally came into being. In the early days of the Church the solitaries came first, and then the monks and nuns. Men were the pioneers, and the women followed. Then out of this monastic life of prayer and mortification sprang the various orders of active religious, raised up one after the other to meet the pressing needs of the time.

We, on the other hand, started in the revival by first recovering the active life—Sisters of Charity devoted to the poor and sick. Then came other active Sisters for the purposes of educational, preventive and rescue work. After that the men followed— mission priests and lay Brothers, communities of men for training ordinands, for the care of aged and infirm sailors, and for the "downs and outs", etc., etc. And most of these communities of men and women have spread out into the mission field.

Now we discover that, quietly and without observation, enclosed nuns have come to life, like the seed hidden and growing secretly in the earth. We find them here just as we suddenly find the flowers in full blossom in the garden, without seeing them unfold. There is yet awaited, last of all, the coming of enclosed monks as of men born out of due time. Then we shall have completely recovered.

Until the enclosed monks are born to us the power of the Church is seriously weakened. We suffer because of the absence of their lives of prayer and mortification—the two most essential implements needed in the terrific warfare for God against the world, the flesh and the devil. The Church is waiting for such lives—waiting for you, young men, because you are strong, and the Word of God abideth in you, and you have overcome the wicked one, you who can ensure that there are men as well as women always standing by night and day to praise the Lord.

Without such monks we are in grave danger of losing sight of the fact that there are some things God has set the Church to do for Him that can only be accomplished by prayer and mortification. Is it not precisely to this purpose of prayer and mortification our Lord was referring when He said to His disappointed disciples, " this kind goeth not out except by prayer and fasting "?

God's arm is not shortened. Somewhere among us are those to whom God is waiting to impart this rare vocation. And we ask for your prayers during this centenary year, that He will graciously impart it now; and that they to whom this call shall come will fully and courageously respond to it; and that, please God, once again the desert will shoot out her blossoms and restore to the Church these specialists in prayer and mortification, monks as well as nuns, monks who will, like Moses on the mountain-top, stretch forth their hands in strong and never-failing supplications while those on the plains beneath continue their heroic activities.

Who can doubt that we, too, shall then prevail? It will be the breaking of a new day. With the help of our God, we shall leap over the wall.

God bless you.

THE nobility of Father William's venture at Glasshampton and the heroism of his perseverance received such wide recognition that one has been tempted not to discuss the question of the regularity of his position. But this merits discussion because of the vital issues that it raises, questions of real importance for the future development of the Religious Life in England.

One would not seek to deny that the character of his position as a Religious was one without precedent since the recovery of the life of religious communities in the Church of England nor that it was to some extent an anomalous one. The Church of England is so constituted that pioneers in the restoration of the Religious Life have been as often as not placed in some such position. The centralisation of the Church of Rome and the relative omnipotence of the Supreme Pontiff in some ways ease the position for the Religious in that Church who is striving to do what Father William sought to do in ours. Had Father William been a Roman Catholic his position with relation to his community, his diocese and the Church in general would have been clarified by a formal " indult " letter of " extra-claustra-tion " or of " secularisation ". A perusal of canons 497, 597, 608, 639 of the new canon law will make clear the principles and conditions governing such a position.

I do not know whether or not Father William had studied the new common law: in any case, these newly revised statutes could not be regarded as governing the behaviour of an Anglican com-munity. But he had a very deep regard for Catholic order, and for the honour of the " religious state ". He always sought the wisest and best-informed counsel that was accessible to guide him in his delicate problems. As a matter of fact, his behaviour was in conformity with the principles embodied in canons 497, 608, 639. But he himself would have referred to the more ancient law of Innocent III (Anno 1212), which he had studied in Father Arthur Devine's chapter on the " commutation of vows " in the book

Convent Life (p. 171, 4th ed., Washbourne, 1877). "This transfer", says the Pontiff, "should not be denied to him who is led to ask for it with humility and purity of intention, that he may not feignedly (ficte) but really pass to the pasture of a better life. Such an one after he has asked the permission to pass to a stricter life from his Prelate, may freely carry out his resolution notwithstanding any indiscreet opposition on the part of the Prelate. . . . Let no one presume under any occasion to forsake the Prelacy."

This constitution speaks of transference from one religious institute to another. The difficulty in Father William's case was, that there was in the Church of England no such stricter institute leading the life to which he believed himself to be called, though many who are in positions of responsibility in the religious life desire that there should be. It was in the full realisation of this predicament that the Superior General of S.S.J.E. and the Superior of S.D.C. formulated the principles which they regarded as governing his future. He was therefore *conditionally* released, though this phrase was never used by himself or his community, to live the enclosed life in the hope that this would lead to the foundation of an enclosed order.

His dismissal to this work was not given till he was nearly fifty-seven years old; and in striving to expedite it he had pleaded very strongly with the community, as reasons against delay, not only his advanced age, but the many years it would take for any house of the sort designed to be set on foot. It is therefore not astonishing that, despite continual failure and disappointment, he did not ask to be allowed to return to live with his community. He twice asked counsel about this, and was advised not to do so.

There was never any time until just before his death that he was not in correspondence with men who looked forward to testing their vocation at Glasshampton. It is true that towards the end he was dissuading men from doing so and sending them to established communities. But there was always in his mind the possibility of the gift of some soul with an inexpugnable vocation to the enclosed life who should be sent by God to complete his work.

The hermit-life to which he resigned himself in his last months at Glasshampton, he regarded as his last contribution towards the purpose for which his community had sent him forth.

The Warden of S.D.C. at one time advised the Superior of the

community to recall Father William. His view is certainly
defensible in view of the hard times which the community had
from time to time to endure owing to the loss of priest-brethren.
But the community decided against recalling him. Their wisdom
is surely a matter of thanksgiving.

APPENDIX III

THE FUTURE OF GLASSHAMPTON

AT the end of the September following upon Father William's
death the solicitors of Mr. Alex Comley, the new owner of the
Glasshampton estate, intimated to the executors of Father
William that Mr. Comley was willing to consider the sale of
the monastery, providing that the property should be secured
for Religious purposes only.

The executors sent out an appeal saying it was proposed that
the monastery should be purchased as a memorial to Father
William. This met with a very generous response, and on
June 28th, 1938, the conveyance was signed placing Glasshampton in the hands of a company, set up for trustee purposes
only, which would hold Glasshampton until such times as it
should again become the home of a monastic House of men.

The monastery and the small portion of land upon which it
stood, together with water supply, drainage and right-of-way,
was bought for £2000. The balance of the appeal was invested
in 3% War Stock in the names of the trustees.

So was fulfilled Father William's hope and trust that the
monastery would be preserved as a Religious Foundation. For
its Life continues. This second beginning of Community Life
had of necessity to be suspended at the outbreak of war in 1939,
and the monastery left in the hands of caretakers. . It has now
been reopened. Priests have returned, and the Life of Prayer and
Reparation is being offered at Glasshampton as in Father William's
time.

At the time of the printing of the second edition brethren of
the Society of Saint Francis whose mother-house is The Friary,
Cerne Abbas, are at Glasshampton guarding the life of the
monastery.

EPILOGUE

By the REVEREND R. E. RAYNES,
Superior of the Community of the Resurrection.

THE rite of the Ordination of Priests in the Book of Common Prayer, by the language which is used, lays very great emphasis upon the pastoral duties of the priest. No doubt there were good reasons—the fruit of past experience—which led to this; but equally there is little doubt that this emphasis has tended to a one-sided conception of, and attitude towards, the priesthood and to the obscuring of the more directly Godward side of the priestly life. The statement that " the sole end of priesthood is the contemplation of the divine " might be said to be an exaggeration in the opposite direction. Nevertheless it is nearer the truth than the suggestion that pastoral activity is the primary duty of the priest. A fruitful pastorate springs from an interior life of contemplation of and communion with God. Of priests above all others one ought to be able to say that their life is hidden with Christ in God. If, after the example of Christ, we are rightly to minister to men, we must begin where He begins by glorifying the Father. This is true of the whole of the Church, which is the priestly body. It is especially true of the ordained ministry, who must habitually be looking to God so that all men may follow their example. Like Jesus the great High-priest " they are to be merciful and faithful priests in the things pertaining unto God ". This truth is one which is perpetually in danger of being obscured in the Anglican Communion. As the Bishop of Bradford wrote in his preface to Fr. William's book ' Watchman—What of the Night? ', " Our church is busy and energetic but her spiritual temperature is not yet as warm as it might be. The whole trend of our times is towards what has been called ' the heresy of good works ' ".

The Oxford Movement was in its beginning concerned with the recovery and reassertion of doctrine long submerged beneath a sea of ignorance and misunderstanding. This bore fruit in the

Catholic revival in the parishes of England, led by priests of out-standing pastoral and evangelistic zeal. And side by side with this there came the revival of the Religious Life. Fr. William says " let us pause a moment to notice the curious fact that in the recovery of this life (*sic*—the Religious Life) by the Anglican Communion, the order in which it grew up in the first instance within the early Church has been entirely reversed ". It was from the solitaries and the hermits that there sprung up the com-munities of monks and nuns and it was from them in turn that there came into being other forms of the Religious Life—techni-cally known as the Mixed life and the Active life. In the restoration of the Religious Life in the Anglican Communion the reverse has been true. Communities of men and women have come into being bound by the vows of Religion, following the evangelical counsels and given to great works of teaching and preaching, bearing heavy burdens in the mission field, caring for the sick and the aged, helping the fallen and succouring the oppressed. And after them, quietly and unobserved, have come societies of Enclosed Nuns—following the life of contemplation. The ordin-ary faithful member of the English Church probably does not know as much as he ought about the Religious Life and its place in the life of the Church, and what he does know is usually de-rived from some acquaintance with an " Active Order ". The monastic life is to him a closed book, or else dismissed as being " useless " because outwardly it " does nothing ". The fact is that the Contemplative life—the life given directly to God in adoration and silence centred upon the recitation of the divine office and the altar—is essential to the completeness of the Re-ligious Life, the three expressions of which (the Contemplative, the Mixed and the Active) are complementary the one to the others. Their difference lies not in the nature of the life, but in the direction of its intention. An even more important factor is that all three expressions of the Religious Life are necessary to the completeness of the Mystical Body of Christ, His Church, because prayer and action are not alternatives. " The most active life must be steeped in prayer—the most solitary is to be lived actively on behalf of the whole mystic body." Nor may we draw distinctions as to the value of these differing vocations, nor try to place them in order of merit. Vocations are calls from God to be obeyed, not argued about. Each is dependent upon and interwoven with the other, and each must be what

God wills them to be. If this somewhat lengthy explanation is intelligible, it should go far to help us understand Fr. William and what he was guided to do. He would be the first to admit that the Religious Life in all its forms is necessary to the well being of the Church on earth. He would be the last to suggest that we are to draw invidious distinctions between activity and contemplation. The very record of his life proves this— a zealous parish priest, a member of a Religious society given to pastoral and charitable works, and finally following the way of contemplation practically alone. His writings also bear testimony to this truth. "There is", he writes, "the way of Martha and the way of Mary. Sometimes these two ways are found combined in the same life. It is thus that God has constituted the services of men as well as those of angels in a wonderful order". Here he sets forth the three expressions of the Religious Life as constituted by God Himself and bids the Church give thanks that two have been by the mercy of God restored to our Communion and abundantly blessed. But the Contemplative life in our midst was in his day (and still is much the same) a tender plant beside the flowering tree of the Active life and the Mixed life. He saw most clearly that such a way of life was necessary not only to the Religious communities but to the whole Church. His own words are the best on the subject. "The absence of any one of these many ways of life mars the Church's fullest resemblance to the life of the Incarnate Son of God wherein all forms of life are perfectly exemplified. Until *enclosed monks living the contemplative life* are raised up for us the life of the Church is incomplete and its power of interceding with God is weakened. We suffer because of the absence of their lives of prayer and mortification. . . ."

This was the vision which he saw with the eyes of his mind and the eyes of his soul. It was a heavenly vision and like St. Paul he could not be disobedient to it. It constrained and compelled him to embark upon the adventure of Glasshampton. We cannot understand the strange record of that adventure unless we understand that. Many would "write it off" as a failure, but no such simple obedience or selfless sacrifice is without fruit. God is giving and will give much increase to the little seed planted by Fr. William. The Cross itself was—and still is— "written off" as a failure, yet it is the tree of life and the fountain of living waters.

The words "simple obedience" and "selfless sacrifice" were deliberately chosen because they explain Fr. William and many of the perplexing things about him. There is here the risk of presumption on the part of the writer in trying to analyse Fr. William with whom he was not personally acquainted, but I venture to say that what stands out pre-eminently in his life is his simplicity and his humility. There is little doubt that he had climbed the ladder of humility as it is set forth in the Rule of St. Benedict, and this produced that selflessness. His life at Glasshampton centred round the Liturgy, the Office and silent contemplation of God—a life of prayer and interior mortification : the two great weapons, as he called them, for gaining the victory in the incessant warfare against the spirit of the age and the temptations of the world, the flesh and the devil. And behind all this was his complete simplicity which led him step by step to the fulfilment of his vocation. As one who knew him intimately wrote—" He just believed in God and knew God and everything followed from that."

Unfortunately the word simplicity has, in modern usage, become degraded to such an extent that now when we speak of a " simple " person, we may easily be interpreted to mean one who is mentally defective. But in its true meaning simplicity is the opposite of duplicity and means single-mindedness as opposed to double-mindedness. St. James tells us that a double-minded man is unstable in all his ways. A single-minded man is neither a fool nor a fanatic. He is a man who clearly sees the end and purpose of his life and subordinates everything to that end. Our Lord explains the result of single-mindedness— " If thine eye be single thy whole body shall be full of light ". The results of this simplicity of heart are clearly to be seen in Fr. William's life. In the first place it gave to him a clarity of vision as to the place and need of the Contemplative life in the Church and the certainty of his own vocation to such a life. This accounts for his quiet, humble and patient determination. He readily obeyed the direction of his superiors and with resignation to the will of God accepted delays and obstacles, but he *knew* that he could not, must not, be disobedient to the heavenly vision. Secondly, his simplicity enabled him to understand the complexities of the world. He had not only seen the world, he had seen through it. So he could help, encourage, advise and direct so many souls bewildered by the trammels of this naughty world. He showed again, what is so clear in the history of the Church, that it is to those whose mind and heart are ever turned to God that souls in distress and doubt will turn. For like his Lord and Master, he spoke as one with authority—the authority of the knowledge of God. Thirdly, and this is in some ways a puzzling fact, it was his very simplicity that made it so difficult for others to live with him. This simple directness of approach is disconcerting to those who have not yet understood or themselves arrived at it. It may be a legitimate criticism of Fr. William that he did not always realize that those who came to Glasshampton to test their vocations were not as simple as himself and that they had to grow into it. Doubtless he himself sometimes wondered why they did not stay. Great, single-minded persons are often not easy to live with, much as we may love and respect them. But such are the pioneers—such blaze the trail which others will follow when they catch the vision. We believe that in the eyes of God Fr. William was not a failure—we are beginning to know that in the opinion of many he was a pillar of light in the Church. This biography will serve to keep his memory green and to remind us of the importance of those things to which his life bears witness. His full biography will be many spiritual sons (may it be at Glasshampton) following in his steps the path of prayer and mortification. " Can it be that this extraordinary and amazing recovery of the Religious Life shall be allowed to tarry in its onward course for lack of men to carry it forward to its maturity? We believe not."

Feast of the Epiphany, 1946. RAYMOND RAYNES, C.R.